KU-020-518

God's Just Demands

A Commentary on Jonah, Micah and Nahum

John L Mackay

Christian Focus Publications

© 1993 John L. Mackay
ISBN 1 85792 030 9

Published by
Christian Focus Publications Ltd
Geanies House, Fearn, Ross-shire,
IV20 1TW, Scotland, Great Britain.

Printed and bound in Great Britain by
Cox & Wyman Ltd, Reading, Berkshire

Cover design by Donna Macleod

The main Scripture version used is the New International Version
(NIV), © International Bible Society, 1973, 1978, 1984.
Published by Hodder and Stoughton.
Other versions referred to are the Authorised Version (AV), the New
American Standard Bible (NASB) and the New King James Version
(NKJV).

All rights reserved. No part of this publication may be reproduced,
stored in a retrieval system, or transmitted, in any form or by any
means, electronic, mechanical, photocopying, recording or otherwise without the prior permission of Christian Focus Publications.

CONTENTS

NAHUM

MAJOR EVENTS AND REIGNS, 931-586 B.C.

	ISRAEL	JUDAH	ASSYRIA
931 Division of the Kingdom			
900 B.C.			
860-874 Ministry of ELIJAH 853 Battle of QARQAR	Omri 885-874 Ahab 874-853		
850-795 Ministry of ELISHA			
800 B.C.	Jeroboam II 793-753		
780-755 Ministry of JONAH		Uzziah 792-740	
722 Fall of Samaria		Jotham 750-731 Ahaz 735-715	Tiglath - Pileser III 745-727
715-690 Ministry of MICAH 701 Siege of Jerusalem **700 B.C.**		Hezekiah 715-686	Sennacherib 705-681
663 Sack of Thebes 655-635 Ministry of NAHUM		Manasseh 686-642	Esarhaddon 681-669 Ashurbanipal 669-623
		Josiah 640-609	
612 Fall of Nineveh **600 B.C.**			Sin-shar-ishkun 623-612 Ashur-uballit 612-608
586 Fall of Jerusalem			

KINGS OF ISRAEL	KINGS OF JUDAH	KINGS OF ASSYRIA
Omri 885-874	Uzziah 792-740	Shalmaneser III 858-824
Ahab 874-853	Jotham 750-731	Shamsi-Adad V 824-810
Ahaziah 853-852	Ahaz 735-715	Adad-nirari III 810-782
Joram 852-841	Hezekiah 729-686	Shalmaneser IV 782-773
Jehu 841-814	Manasseh 696-642	Ashur-dan III 773-754
Jehoahaz 814-798	Amon 642-640	Adad-nirari V 754-745
Jehoash 798-782	Josiah 640-609	Tiglath-pileser III 745-727
Jeroboam II 793-753	Jehoahaz 609	Shalmaneser V 727-722
Zechariah 753	Jehoiakim 608-598	Sargon II 722-705
Shallum 752	Jehoiachin 598-597	Sennacherib 705-681
Menahem 752-742	Zedekiah 597-586	Esarhaddon 681-669
Pekahiah 742-740		Ashurbanipal 669-626
Pekah 752-732		Ashur-etil-ilani 626-623
Hoshea 732-722		Sin-shum-lishir 623
		Sin-shar-ishkun 623-612
		Ashur-uballit 612-608

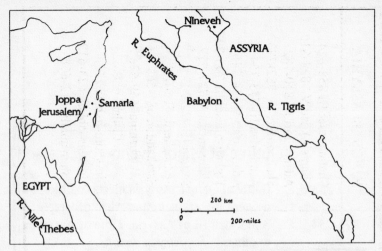

I. Map of Ancient Near East

II. Map of Palestine

Outline of Major Events

853 B.C.	Battle of Qarqar: Assyria meets coalition of western forces, including Ahab of Israel.
773-754 B.C.	Ashur-dan III of Assyria. Time of Assyrian weakness. *Ministry of Jonah.*
745-727 B.C.	Tiglath-Pileser III of Assyria. Resurgence of Assyrian power.
722 B.C.	Fall of Samaria. End of Northern Kingdom of Israel.
715-690 B.C.	*Ministry of Micah.*
705-681 B.C.	Sennacherib of Assyria threatens Jerusalem in 701 B.C.
663 B.C.	Capture of Thebes in Egypt. Height of Assyrian power.
Between 655 and 635 B.C.	*Ministry of Nahum.*
612 B.C.	Fall of Nineveh. Rise of Babylonians.
586 B.C.	Fall of Jerusalem.

Preface

It is not easy to know God. What is more, it can be uncomfortable to live knowing God. But knowing God is essential. 'Now this is eternal life: that they may know you, the only true God, and Jesus Christ, whom you have sent' (John 17:3). We must avoid the danger of corrupting our knowledge of God by substituting a human caricature of what God should be like for the revelation he has given in Scripture of what he really is. It is easy to be influenced by the ideas that exist of God as well-intentioned, undemanding, ready to accept us and give us what we want, and happy to make do with whatever we can scrape together to offer him of our time, resources and affection. Such a sentimental picture is plausible because it is effectively shaped by our sinful, human ideas, and lets us go on living as we please.

These three books of Scripture act as an effective antidote to diminishing God by bringing him down to the sort of being we find it easy to live with. There is no doubt that the only true God is one who does abound in love (Jonah 4:2) and delights to show mercy (Micah 7:18). The prophecy of Jonah ends with the LORD asking his reluctant prophet, 'Should I not be concerned about that great city?' (Jonah 4:11). But we have to learn that God's love and his concern, which encompass even a heathen city, are only one aspect of his character. We must also know him as the one who 'will not leave the guilty unpunished' (Nahum 1:3). We have not really grasped who God is until we realise that living with him has to be done on his terms, not ours. As the Creator of all, he has the right to demand how we live. As the Judge of all, he will exercise his right to demand that we account for what we have done. Knowing God as he really is leads us to acknowledge his just demands on us.

This is seen at various levels in these three short prophetic books. In Jonah, there is the matter of the personal demand made on the prophet. God requires individual obedience, even when the task is one which we do not understand, or with which we are out of sympathy. Disobedience merits God's judgment and wrath. There is also the divine demand for obedience from Nineveh. The pagan city at the heart of a great empire was not exempt from God's requirements and scrutiny, for he rules over all the kingdoms of mankind. If Nineveh had not changed her ways, she would have been engulfed by divine judgment.

In Micah, the focus is on the LORD's demands on his own people of Judah. They had been the recipients of God's favour, and he had entered into covenant with them. They were the ones whose lives should have been a living expression of their allegiance and gratitude. But they were not, and so Micah summoned them to consider and amend their ways which were out of alignment with God's covenant demands. If they did not repent, God would justly punish them. That would not, however, be God's last word about his chosen people. After they had been punished for their rebellion, God would again extend mercy to them.

In Nahum, the demands of God's justice fall on Nineveh. Well over a century had elapsed from the days of Jonah, and Nineveh had reverted to its former cruelty. In the destruction that overwhelmed the once proud and self-confident city, there is a solemn reminder to all the nations of the earth that God will demand that they answer for their conduct before his judgment seat.

All of human life is subject to the requirements that God imposes on it. We have a fatally flawed view of him if we expect that he is unaware of our conduct, or indifferent to it. There is no ultimate evasion of his just demands on us. Since all have sinned and failed to live up to the demands of God (Romans 3:9-23), the final destiny of humanity would inevitably have been one of eternal punishment, had not God spontaneously and graciously provided a remedy. Salvation is possible only because God has permitted the penalty of his judgment to fall on a substitute, his own Son. He paid the price in the place of his people. It is only in this way that the demands of God's justice could be met and salvation provided for fallen humanity. Eternal life involves not only knowing and acknowledging God's just demands, but also knowing Jesus Christ, whom the Father sent, as the one who can effectively deal with the situation that arises when we fail to meet those demands.

JONAH

Overview

Jonah is different from the other eleven works that have been gathered in the collection we know as the Minor Prophets. It alone does not principally consist of the messages delivered by the prophets. The book of Jonah is a narrative, and has many resemblances to the narratives about Elijah and Elisha recorded in the Books of Kings. Indeed, Jonah was their successor. Elijah died in 847 B.C., and Elisha's ministry can be dated around 850-795 B.C. Jonah was probably a younger contemporary of Elisha, who outlived him. Little information is given about the date of his ministry, but his visit to Nineveh seems to fall in the period 780-755 B.C.

Like the narratives about Elijah and Elisha, the miraculous features prominently in the book of Jonah. This has led many to challenge its historicity. Undoubtedly it is not written as modern history. It omits many names and facts that we would have expected to be included. But they were not relevant for the purposes of the narrator. We may compare this with the number of times in Kings when the specific monarch with whom Elisha is dealing is left quite unnamed (2 Kings 5,7). The same terse narrative style is found in both places, focusing on what the narrator wants to emphasise as the point of the story. But such compactness and selectivity do not make Jonah unfactual, any more than does the presence of miracles – unless we have previously decided that miracles cannot happen anyway. Those who adopt that perspective are going to have trouble accepting most of Scripture, which prominently displays God's power not only in creating, but also in superintending his creation.

We shall also note that, apart from the miracles, there are other features of the narrative that have led many to question the historicity of Jonah. But there are more than adequate explanations that may be advanced to counter such doubts. There is no good reason to suppose that this book is a fable or a parable. It is undoubtedly a story that can teach us much, but that is because it really happened. It is not due to the fertile imagination of some masterly story-teller. Since there is no formal indication of the author of this book, we cannot be certain who it actually was, but much of the information must have come from Jonah himself, and it may well have been written by him, or someone very close to him.

The main purpose of the book was to stir Israel up to consider the character of the LORD whom they professed to serve, and to examine the nature of their relationship to him. That was why the story was written and included in the canon of Scripture. Jonah's mission to Nineveh was divinely designed to make Israel jealous, as the LORD displayed how he could bless a heathen nation. As is brought out in the concluding verse (4:11), Jonah himself had to learn about God's concern for all mankind, whether Jew or Gentile. But though Jonah is a short book, its teaching is not confined to one theme. Jonah's own experience was a much-needed warning against disobedience, as well as a display of divine grace claiming and restoring the sinner, even as he defiantly tries to evade God's command.

The chapter divisions correspond with the structure of the book. There are two sections, chapters 1 and 2, and chapters 3 and 4, both of which have a similar pattern. They begin with the prophet receiving the LORD's commission and his reaction to it (1:1-3; 3:1-4). The consequences of the prophet's actions are then related (1:4-16; 3:5-9): first the storm caused by his disobedience; and then when he obeys God and brings his message to Nineveh, the repentance displayed in that city. Both 1:17 and 3:10 are transitional verses that bridge between what has gone before and what follows, by relating how the LORD intervenes sovereignly in the situation to save. Jonah's reaction to this is then related: in the first instance, his own gratitude at being saved (chapter 2), but later his hostility at the LORD's relenting towards Nineveh (4:1-4). This leads into a final section (4:4-11) where the LORD acts to straighten out the prophet's attitudes and thinking.

Jonah 1:1-3: I Must Get Away From This!

The story of Jonah is narrated simply and effectively. Details we might want to know about are omitted because they would only divert attention from what should be grasped. This terse style is found right from the start, where in the first three verses we are introduced to Jonah (1:1), told of his commission (1:2), and of his disobedience (1:3). The story of the runaway prophet who feels he must get away from the LORD's command matches in its breathless style the breathlessness Jonah must have experienced when he arrived at Joppa. To appreciate all that is being said we have to look at it more slowly.

The word of the LORD came to (*verse 1*) is a phrase found over 100 times in the Old Testament to describe what took place when the LORD spoke to one of his prophets. Generally it is followed by the message they were authorised to deliver to the people in the name of the LORD. This is found, for instance, at the beginning of the prophecies of Joel and Micah. But there are also passages, such as this, where what is related is a set of instructions to the prophet himself, as, for example to Elijah in 1 Kings 17:2; 21:17. It is the LORD's initiative that gets the story of Jonah started, just as it is the LORD's hand that determines the outcome.

The prophet who receives the LORD's message is named as **Jonah son of Amittai**. Some have felt that because the name Jonah means 'a dove', and Amittai is connected with the Hebrew word for 'truth' or 'truthfulness', an allegorical interpretation of the book is justified. This, however, is being too fanciful. Hebrew names nearly always meant something (just as Brown or Smith do), and Jonah here is just a name. We are told he is Jonah son of Amittai, because he is a real person about whom more is known from 2 Kings 14:23-27.

Jonah's prophetic ministry coincided with the reign of Jeroboam II (793-753 B.C.), who ruled over the northern kingdom of Israel. It had broken away from Judah after the death of Solomon (931 B.C.), and its subsequent history was marked by spiritual decline and apostasy. First of all, a debased worship of the LORD using idols and a non-Levitical priesthood had been established in the north, but by the time of Elijah's ministry (around 860-847 B.C.) the land had degenerated to outright worship of the Canaanite god, Baal. Though this threat had been dealt with by Elijah, and also by Jeroboam II's great-grandfather, Jehu (2 Kings 10:18-29), the official religion of the northern kingdom continued to be corrupted by idolatry and paganism. This was still true under Jeroboam II (2 Kings 14:24).

But Jonah was given an extraordinary message regarding Jeroboam's reign. It was going to be a time of prosperity and national success (2 Kings 14:25). This was not a reward for Jeroboam's piety, or that of his people. It was rather a gracious initiative from the LORD. Because of their disloyalty, he had been punishing his people through foreign invasion from both Syria (Aram) and Assyria, but now, seeing their desperate circumstances – they were on the point of being wiped out – 'he saved them by the hand of Jeroboam' (2 Kings 14:26,27). Repeated defeat before their enemies had not brought the people to their senses, and unfortunately granting a predicted time of blessing was to fail also. The people did not recognise their good fortune as coming from the LORD (Hosea 2:8). But knowing that it was Jonah who had brought the message of the coming period of prosperity helps us to understand his thinking in connection with the altogether different message he is commanded to relay in this book.

2 Kings also provides us with the information that Jonah came from Gath-Hepher (2 Kings 14:25; see Map II). In Joshua 19:13 this village is identified as being in the territory of Zebulun, and it probably lay a few miles north of Nazareth. Jonah was the only Old Testament prophet we know about from Galilee (John 7:52), and he is the only Old Testament prophet to whom Jesus compares himself and his ministry (Matt. 12:39-41; Luke 11:29-32; see on 1:17).

In the book of Jonah, however, it is not to his own nation that the prophet has to deliver his message – at least that is how it appears initially. We do have to remember that he wrote this book for them, so what he was doing affected them too. However, what the LORD says to him is **"Go to the great city of Nineveh"** (*verse 2*). In fact it begins with 'Arise!', a word that the NIV does not translate. It is used not just of getting to one's feet, but also of responding speedily to a matter that is presented as urgent. The task that the LORD is assigning to Jonah is one that requires immediate action.

Now Nineveh was in northern Mesopotamia, on the east bank of the river Tigris, opposite the modern city of Mosul (see Map 1). While it was not the capital of Assyria in Jonah's day, it was a major centre with royal palaces where the king would on occasion stay. It was a large and wealthy city, benefiting from Assyria being the major power in Mesopotamia. Its size and importance are mentioned again in 3:3 and 4:11. Jonah was being ordered to go to a major pagan metropolis.

Assyria had spread its power throughout the Near East. Already there had been various contacts with Israel. Assyrian records tell us that in 853 B.C. Ahab king of Israel was one of an alliance of western states that fought against the Assyrian king Shalmaneser III at Qarqar. Assyrian records again tell us that in 841 Jehu paid tribute to Shalmaneser III of Assyria. Also in 796 Jehoash paid tribute to Adad-nirari III, who was conducting a series of campaigns in the west, evidently in an attempt to keep the area under his control.

There are other instances of Old Testament prophecies against foreign nations (Obadiah, Jeremiah 46-51), but the prophet did not ordinarily travel to the foreign land to deliver it. The messages against the foreign nations had as their primary function reassuring God's own people of his watchfulness over their affairs and his readiness to act appropriately against those who harassed them.

But here Jonah is to go to Nineveh with a message. **Preach against it, because its wickedness has come up before me**. It is a denunciation of the city from the God who rules all. It proceeds on the basis of the LORD being the one to whom all nations are accountable. Whether they acknowledge him or not, he is 'the Judge of all the earth' (Gen. 18:25), and is taking official cognisance of what they are doing. When he decides to act in the matter, it is inevitable that judgment will engulf the city.

Nineveh was a major centre of the Assyrian Empire. As the Assyrians had increased their zone of influence through the ancient world, they had became renowned for their cruelty and rapaciousness (see on Nahum 3:1). Already this feature of Assyrian power had become so notorious that it called for specific divine intervention. There is no indication that the message to be sent would call for repentance, but that is an inevitable inference. When God warns people of his impending judgment, it is with the aim that they will respond in time and be saved. 'If at any time I announce that a nation or kingdom is to be uprooted, torn down and destroyed, and if that nation I warned repents of its evil, then I will relent and not inflict on it the disaster I had planned' (Jer. 18:7-8).

But what was the reason for God giving this commission to Jonah? One of the lessons of the book is that God's ways are beyond ours, and that his actions are not constrained by our understanding of what is going on. Our capacity to understand and approve does not set the standard to which God has to adhere.

Still there is more to it than that. Fitting it in with the divine programme outlined in 2 Kings, enables us to see that if Jonah had carried out the commission when it was originally given to him, then it would have fulfilled a very important role in God's dealings with his covenant people – namely provoking them to respond to him. This was one aspect of the LORD's procedure in dealing with his people's waywardness and desertion of him. As early as the time of Moses, such circumstances had led him to say, 'I will make them envious by those who are not a people; I will make them angry by a nation that has no understanding' (Deut. 32:21). To rebuke them for their ingratitude, the LORD would make his own people envious of the blessings he had bestowed on others (Rom. 10:19-21; 11:14).

In this respect we can see an element of continuity between Jonah's ministry and that of his immediate predecessors, Elijah and Elisha. They too had been used to bring divine blessing to outsiders. Elijah had been ordered to go to Zarephath in Sidonian (Phoenician) territory, and had provided food for a widow and her family and restored her son to life (1 Kings 17). Elisha had cured Naaman the Syrian of his leprosy (2 Kings 5). Such facts did not sit comfortably with the small-minded view of the scope of divine blessing held by the Jews of our Lord's day (Luke 4:24-30). It is quite likely that Jonah and his generation considered themselves to have an exclusive right to the LORD's favour.

The LORD was blessing Israel with respite from their enemies, but this was so that they would return to him. It would not have been long after this that the LORD would send Amos and Hosea to Israel to condemn them for their ingratitude and lack of response. Jonah's ministry presumably took place earlier in Jeroboam's reign, and was designed to urge them back to the LORD, by showing how Nineveh would respond to the blessing bestowed on it (Matt. 12:41; 11:20-24).

But matters did not develop in such a straightforward fashion. Having received his urgent commission, one would have expected the narrative to have continued, 'And Jonah arose and went to Nineveh.' That's the way other prophets responded (e.g. Elijah, in 1 Kings 17:9,10), and it's the way Jonah will respond eventually too (3:3) – but first there's a rather surprising detour. **But Jonah ran away from the LORD and headed for Tarshish** (*verse 3*). That was in the opposite direction. To get to Nineveh, Jonah would have had to travel north and then east. We are not sure where he was when he received the command. Presumably it was in the Northern Kingdom, though perhaps not at his home town of Gath-Hepher. Had he been there, the port he could have reached soonest would have been Acco, which lay further north than Joppa (see Map II). It is likely that he was in the south of the land, not far from the capital, Samaria.

The location of Tarshish is uncertain. The word means a 'refinery' or 'smelter', and was used of a number of sites around the Mediterranean where Phoenicians traders had gone to find metals. The most probable situation for it is in what is now southern Spain, near the mouth of the Guadalquivir. Scripture views it as a distant and remote place (Psalm 72:10; Isa. 66:19). Jonah's choice is thus seen to be of somewhere as far as possible from the city to which he had been directed to go.

Two questions are raised by this. (1) Why did Jonah not want to obey the command? (2) Did he really expect to change anything by running away?

(1) We are not told at this point the reasons for Jonah's disobedience. That remains until later (4:2). But his response does not seem to have been motivated by the personal danger involved. Undoubtedly taking an unpopular message to Nineveh was no easy matter, but Jonah's attitude later on (1:12; 4:3,8) does not suggest that he was particularly afraid of death. Jonah did not want the LORD to spare Nineveh. He understood the conditional nature of the command given to him. It was opening up the possibility of a positive response from the people of Nineveh, and that would mean that the enemies of his people – and the enemies of God – would be blessed. Jonah's problems were primarily theological. Having already been the means of delivering a message of prosperity to his own people, he did not want to be party to a revival of Assyrian fortunes. They were pagan and had already shown their hostility to the LORD. They were only worthy of judgment. God should preserve the line of distinction between his own people whom he blesses and others who rejected him and should be rejected.

(2) As regards how his running away would solve his problems, there may have been an element of unthinking, irrational response, induced by guilt. He knew he was in the wrong and, like Adam and Eve trying to hide from the presence of the LORD among the trees of the garden (Gen. 3:8), he just wanted to avoid the one he had offended. It is unlikely that Jonah really believed he could find somewhere that the LORD's writ did not run. He himself will shortly confess (1:9) that the LORD is God of heaven and earth. He never doubted that, or believed that one could escape the scrutiny of God (Jer. 23:24). As chapter 2 shows, Jonah was conversant with the Psalms, and would have known the words of David, 'Where can I

go from your Spirit? Where can I flee from your presence?' Even
settling 'on the far side of the sea' would not suffice (Psalm
139:7,9).

Why run away then? The key is in the phrase which may be
literally rendered 'Jonah arose to flee to Tarshish from the presence
of the LORD'. 'The presence of the LORD' was something particularly associated with the land of promise. It was there God had been
pleased to reveal himself to his people. Being there before the LORD
was the place of the prophet's duty. Going somewhere else, away
from the LORD's land and people, Jonah might well have been
hoping that he would have escaped from this commission. It was
not that he thought himself indispensable in carrying out God's
purposes. Rather he thought that by getting out he would not have
to witness what would happen when what was envisaged came to
pass through some other prophet.

The story continues with the first of three mentions of Jonah
'going down', that chart the prophet's disobedience: *going down to
Joppa* (1:3), *going down below deck* (1:5), *going down into the
depths* (2:6). The course of disobedience is downwards until the
LORD intervenes. **He went down to Joppa, where he found a ship
bound for that port. After paying the fare, he went aboard and
sailed for Tarshish to flee from the LORD.** Joppa does not seem
to have been conquered by Israel during Old Testament times, and
so in a sense by going there Jonah would already have half-escaped.
The ship going from Joppa would have been Phoenician. It is a
measure of his desperation to get away that he resorted to going by
sea. The Hebrews were not naturally sailors. The repetition of the
phrase 'to Tarshish away from the presence of the LORD' re-
emphasises Jonah's intention to be quit of the LORD's service.

Jonah 1:4-6: It's Not That Simple
So far Jonah has been allowed to go on his way unhindered. No
doubt he thought it favoured his scheme that he found a ship going
where he wanted. But now the LORD is no longer content to be a

passive spectator of Jonah's disobedience and rebellion. The repetition of 'LORD' at the end of 1:3 and the beginning of 1:4 (they are successive words in the original) strongly emphasises the change that comes about through his intervention.

Then the LORD sent a great wind on the sea (*verse 4*). It is not the ordinary word for 'send' that is used, but a word meaning 'throw', or 'hurl', that is later used of the cargo being thrown into the sea (1:5) and Jonah also (1:15). The LORD whom all things serve (Psalm 119:91) hurled a wind at the sea. The divine control of the sea was a constant theme of Israel's praise (Psalms 24:2; 33:7; 89:9). The mythology of surrounding nations viewed the sea as a primeval force which had to be placated, but Israel asserted that the LORD had created the sea and as Creator he exercised rightful lordship over it. 'He spoke and stirred up a tempest that lifted high the waves' (Psalm 107:25). That is what happens here. **And such a violent storm arose that the ship threatened to break up**. It was no chance occurrence that engulfed Jonah, but the sea at the LORD's bidding acts as his instrument of punishment to find out and discipline the reluctant prophet.

But Jonah was not on his own. His guilt brought awesome consequences on others. Our actions impinge on the lives of others, 'for none of us lives to himself alone' (Rom. 14:7). There is no reason to suppose the 'great storm' was so localised that only one ship was involved, but it is on that one ship the story focuses. **All the sailors were afraid** (*verse 5*). The fear of the sailors is one of the themes of this chapter. It moves on from the natural reaction to their peril (as in Psalm 107:26,27), to an awe-stricken bewilderment at the revelation of Jonah's impiety (1:10), and then to wonder and dread as they recognise the LORD's power (1:16). Their reaction may have been intensified because of the unexpected nature of the storm. Generally there was a closed season for ocean going voyages in the Mediterranean, when storms were likely to occur (Acts 27:9-12). So the seamen would have known that this storm was exceptional not only from its great ferocity, but also by its being out of season.

The crew would probably have been principally Phoenician. The Phoenicians were of Canaanite descent, and occupied roughly the area of modern Lebanon. They were renowned for their maritime activities, trading extensively around the Mediterranean coast, and founding many settlements, the most famous of these being Carthage, which later became the great enemy of Rome. This widespread activity no doubt meant that their ships also recruited crew from the other peoples they encountered.

Aware that this was no ordinary storm, **each cried out to his own god**. Although they were polytheists believing that there were many gods, the heathen often considered themselves to be worshippers of one guardian deity in particular, perhaps the god of their own nation, or birthplace, or one to whom they attributed their past good fortune. Such a patron deity would be expected to accord special favour to his or her own devotees, and would be approached for help in difficult circumstances. Even in pagan thought there remained a consciousness of powers higher than humanity.

But they did not just engage in prayer. **And they threw the cargo into the sea to lighten the ship**. No doubt a trading ship left port heavily laden. It is a measure of their desperation that they were prepared to jettison the cargo, and probably also any spare tackle – the word in Hebrew is quite general. By getting rid of it 'from upon them', the ship would ride higher in the water, and so perhaps they would escape being swamped.

There was, however, one man on board who was quite unaware of all this frantic activity. The story moves back in time to pick up what Jonah had done. **But Jonah had gone below deck, where he lay down and fell into a deep sleep**. This had happened before the storm arose. Jonah had arrived exhausted after his hurried departure to Joppa and, not wishing to be drawn into conversation with anyone, had found a quiet spot in the ship, probably the sleeping quarters below deck. Physically and spiritually worn out by his experience, he had fallen into a more than ordinarily deep sleep (Gen. 15:12; 1 Sam. 26:12). The movement of the boat seems to have kept him asleep rather than wakening him up. It was not a matter of detachment from the ship's plight or indifference to his own spiritual situation. Quite the opposite. Jonah is totally drained by the course of action he has adopted and by the anxiety and inward tension that has come upon him as a result.

The captain went to him (*verse 6*). It may be that when the seamen had gone below decks to take up the cargo to throw it out, they had come upon their unusual passenger and reported it to the captain, or perhaps the situation had become so serious that the captain himself is helping to shift the cargo. The captain's words are reported tersely, but we should not think of them as brusque. At this point he had no reason to suspect that Jonah was the cause of all his troubles. **How can you sleep?** is a question of amazement that at a time of obvious danger someone could be in such a deep sleep. **Get up and call on your god! Maybe he will take notice of us, and we will not perish**. There is an ironic twist to the narrative. The prophet who had been commanded to 'rise ... call against Nineveh' (1:1, literally) is now exhorted to 'rise, call on your god', from whom he was running away! The captain was expressing his own theology. Certain that the storm had a supernatural origin, perhaps this stranger's god was the one behind it all. He does not assume that this or any other god would unquestionably listen to the prayer of a devotee. After all, the heathen gods were known to act capriciously on occasion, and so might well not be prepared to intervene to prevent the disaster that the captain saw looming. But he expected that every individual had his own god, and no possible source of assistance could be overlooked.

We are not told that Jonah complied with the captain's frantic request. As the narrator is careful to point out the importance of prayer (1:5,14; 2:1,2; 3:8; 4:2), we are probably justified in taking this as a significant omission. It wasn't just being roused out of a deep sleep to face a terrific storm and a heaving ship that made Jonah queasy and befuddled. He who disobeys the LORD has disrupted his fellowship with him, and his prayer life cannot but be affected. The accusations of his own conscience which he was suppressing would have shrivelled up any prayer before it could be uttered. This is the prophet who wants to get away from the presence of the LORD, and to approach him in prayer was not possible without repentance. Jonah's silence and his general conduct at this point contrast sharply with that of Paul in similar circumstances (Acts 27:21-26) because one was walking in God's way while the other had set his face against him. The disobedient prophet cannot act as an effective witness to the LORD, while his rebellion lasts.

Jonah 1:7-10: Found Out

The scene switches back on deck. The sailors have thrown the cargo overboard, but the situation remains dire. They have been forced to the conclusion that the extraordinary storm has not arisen by chance. Their pagan background would have led them to attribute it to the action of the gods, one of whom must be offended. They are unaware of having given offence themselves, and therefore take action to find out who it is that is responsible. **Then the sailors said to each other, "Come, let us cast lots to find out who is responsible for this calamity"** (*verse 7*). 'Lots', originally 'little stones', were made from various materials, and probably shaped like dice. They were used in a variety of procedures throughout the ancient east in divination, trying to ascertain the mind of the gods. The lots probably were used in pairs. Each had faces of dark and light colour. If both fell to expose a dark side, a negative answer was being returned; if light faces were revealed, a positive answer; and if there was one light and one dark, no answer was being given.

Use of lots was not just a pagan practice. Although divination in general was forbidden to Israel (Deut. 18:10,11), the casting of lots was permitted in certain circumstances. It was probably not viewed as an attempt to pry into the future, but rather as a way of bringing one's conduct into conformity with the will of the LORD. Lots were used to allocate the territory of the tribes at the Conquest (Josh. 18:6,8,10), to assign the duties of workers in the Temple (1 Chron. 24:5,31; 25:8; 26:13-16), and to choose the scapegoat (Lev. 16:9,10). There were also occasions on which lots were used to obtain divinely guaranteed knowledge about what had happened in the past. When Jonathan ate food contrary to Saul's command, this was found out by use of lot (1 Sam. 14:42). Lots had probably also been used earlier to uncover Achan as the one who had caused Israel's defeat at Ai (Josh. 7:14-18). But it was always acknowledged that the success of the procedure depended on God. 'The lot is cast into the lap, but its every decision is from the LORD' (Prov. 16:33).

It is a similar procedure the sailors employ here. **They cast lots and the lot fell on Jonah**. An answer is given because of the LORD's overruling. He exposes his runaway prophet as the cause of the storm.

Up to this point it is difficult to assess just how much Jonah was prepared to admit to himself. Doubtless he was inwardly troubled because of his disobedience. However, he was no doubt still justifying his behaviour to himself, that it was right not to want to have anything to do with the strange attitude and plan of God regarding Nineveh. It is not certain that he had yet associated the storm with his personal action. But when the lot indicated him as the party responsible for the storm, he must have re-assessed the situation.

The agitated seamen fire a barrage of questions at Jonah. **So they asked him, "Tell us, who is responsible for making all this trouble for us?"** (*verse 8*). The lot has convinced them that Jonah holds the answer to their questions, but they are uncertain if it is Jonah himself who is at fault. **What do you do?** This may also be understood as, 'What are you doing here?' **Where do you come from? What is your country? From what people are you?** These should not be understood as some sort of immigration question-naire. They were religiously loaded questions. The gods of the heathen were generally deities who were worshipped in specific localities. Knowing Jonah's origins would help them decide which god to pray to, if Jonah were the cause of their troubles. Their questions are quite unlike those that Joshua asked Achan after he had been found out by lot (Josh. 7:19). Their concern is not for Jonah or his relationship with his God, but for their own safety.

As the later parenthesis in 1:10 makes clear, the whole of Jonah's answer is not recorded here. It is just his central confession of faith that is given. **He answered, "I am a Hebrew and I worship the LORD, the God of heaven, who made the sea and the land"** (*verse 9*). Israelites generally identified themselves to others as Hebrews (Gen. 40:15; Exod. 1:19; 3:18), and in certain texts the term is used specifically to distinguish between native Israelites and others (Deut. 15:12). It may not have been such an obvious corollary to say 'and I worship the LORD', because by Jonah's time there was much mixed worship in the land. Undoubtedly Jehu had turned the nation back from the outright paganism which had been the target of Elijah's protests during the reign of Ahab. But the worship of Israel was still syncretistic, an amalgam of worship of the LORD and worship of Baal.

Jonah refers to the LORD as 'the God of heaven'. This title is one that had occurred from earliest times (Gen. 24:3,7), but it became more commonly used in the post-exilic period as the Jews tried to communicate to others the transcendence of their God (Ezra 1:2; Neh. 1:4,5; Dan. 2:18). The name *Yahweh*, rendered as 'the LORD', was a personal name, and would not have meant much to people from other nations. It had to be explained that he was not a god of a certain city, or people, or land. As God of heaven, he is supreme (including being supreme over other gods) and his rule extends everywhere. Jonah also confesses that his God was the Creator who had made the sea and the land (Psalm 95:5), and who therefore was in control of what was happening to them as the tempest raged all around them (Psalm 135:6).

In the telling of the story, it is significant that the word Jonah uses to describe his relation to the LORD, 'worship', is literally 'fear'. This is a common Old Testament term for the true reverence that ought to characterise the worshipper of the LORD (Prov. 1:7), who perceives his exaltation and holiness. It is used here to contrast with the fear felt by the sailors (1:5,10,16). Theirs began as a genuine terror of the circumstances in which they found themselves. But though Jonah's confession of the LORD as his God is orthodox, is it genuine? It could only be a formal confession of loyalty while he was disobedient. (In this there is a parallel with the situation of Israel which professed loyalty to the LORD, but did not match it with obedience. No doubt those for whom this book was written were meant to see that.) The prophet had lost sight of the reality of the God whom he professed to follow. The sailors, however, progress from fear of the storm, to a great fear of what they have become involved in, to a fear that leads them to worship the LORD.

This terrified them (*verse 10*) is literally 'the men feared a great fear'. It was a reaction that exceeded what they felt in the face of the storm that engulfed them. The parenthetical explanation, **They knew he was running away from the LORD, because he had already told them so**, does not refer back to the beginning of the voyage, but to the present interrogation. The narrator is condensing. Jonah had made a complete confession of his situation to the sailors, and by now they know as much as we do. It is therefore with bewilderment and horror that **they asked, "What have you done?"** They could not take in the full dimensions of what Jonah had revealed to them. Rather than expressing a desire for more information, their question was an exclamation of consternation at the enormity of what Jonah had done – something he himself had hitherto failed to grasp.

Though Jonah's conduct had been defiant and rebellious, there is much to be admired in the way he now conducts himself. There is no suggestion that he tries to evade the issue at stake, or to play down his own role. Confronted with the enormity of what he had done and its consequences, he openly acknowledges his fault and admits responsibility.

Jonah 1:11-16: The Drastic Solution

While the sailors' interrogation of Jonah was proceeding, **the sea was getting rougher and rougher** (*verse 11*). They had identified the source of the problem, but more needed to be done to resolve the situation. It was not a problem that the seamen could solve for themselves. In pagan religions it was imperative that each god was approached in the way specified by him – and especially so if the god was angry. They did not know about the worship of Jonah's God, and **so they asked him, "What should we do to you to make the sea calm down for us?"** Jonah, as a prophet of the LORD, was the one who could inform them how to deal with the situation, but they expect that action will have to be taken with respect to Jonah himself. If nothing is done, the storm is going to destroy them all.

"Pick me up and throw me into the sea," he replied, "and it will become calm" (*verse 12*). Jonah's reply is in effect to tell them to surrender him to his God from whom he had been fleeing. He is acknowledging that the LORD would not let him go, and that the sea was acting as the LORD's agent to catch and punish him. Jonah has no doubt that what has happened has been his fault. **I know that it is my fault that this great storm has come upon you.** If it is the LORD seeking him out to punish him, then the matter can only be concluded by that punishment coming upon him, and he acts to avoid others being drawn to their doom along with him. He uses the same word 'throw' as had occurred previously in 1:4 for the LORD sending a great storm, literally 'throwing' it, and in 1:5 for the sailors ineffectually throwing the cargo overboard to lighten the ship. Throwing Jonah into the sea will bring the storm to an end, for the LORD's complaint was not against the ship and its crew, but against his prophet. He is the one who has to face the consequences of his rebellion.

The seamen, however, were not immediately willing to adopt the course of action proposed by Jonah. The consideration shown by the heathen sailors to Jonah after he has confessed his rebellion contrasts sharply with Jonah's subsequent attitude towards Nineveh (4:1). **Instead, the men did their best to row back to land** (*verse 13*). It would seem that Jonah's open behaviour had made an impression on them, and they felt that the drastic course of action he was recommending would be liable to expose them to even greater troubles, as 1:14 indicates. It may be that the storm had

arisen not long after their departure from Joppa, so that to row back
to land was not a course of utter despair. No doubt they had already
tried to do so, but despite their previous lack of success, they try
again, because they want to get rid of Jonah, but not in the way he
had suggested. The LORD, however, thwarted their expedients. **But
they could not, for the sea grew even wilder than before**. What
conditions were like by this time is unimaginable, for hitherto they
had been extraordinarily serious.

**Then they cried to the LORD, "O LORD, please do not let us
die for taking this man's life"** (*verse 14*). They had been afraid to
follow Jonah's indicated course of action, because they were
uncertain how the LORD would respond. **Do not hold us accountable for killing an innocent man**. 'Innocent' does not indicate that
they felt Jonah was being accused unjustly. It is rather a recognition
that they did not constitute a court of justice, and therefore had no
right to put any to death. They do not want to be held accountable
for shedding innocent blood. This was a serious matter in other
lands as well as in Israel (Deut. 21:1-9).

For you, O LORD, have done as you pleased. This introduces
a key theme in the book – the sovereignty of the LORD, and his right
and ability to act, quite apart from the desires and wishes of man
(3:9; 4:11). The sailors are arguing that the LORD had caused the
storm and placed them in the circumstances in which they found
themselves, and therefore no punitive sanctions should be inflicted
on them.

Then they took Jonah and threw him overboard (*verse 15*).
Having presented their case to the LORD, they act as had been
suggested. **And the raging sea grew calm**. The simplicity of the
statement serves to bring out the suddenness and completeness of the
change. It provided them with an awe-inspiring example of the
power of the LORD (Psalm 107:25; Mark 4:41).

At this the men greatly feared the LORD (*verse 16*). Their fear
of the storm and of the circumstances now changes to a fear of the
LORD (1:5,10). It is not suggested, however, that they became
monotheists, and worshipped the LORD exclusively (see on 3:5).

They offered a sacrifice to the LORD and made vows to him. They now took his reality and power into their reckoning. Their sacrifice could have been only of a most minimal sort on board a ship where the cargo, and probably also any superfluous tackling, had been jettisoned. It may be that they waited until they got to land, because sacrifice would ordinarily have been offered at a temple through a priest. Probably when they got back to land, they would have found in Israel a shrine to Yahweh at which to present their offering. The vows would have been regarding the making of future offerings to the LORD. Their new respect for the LORD would not be a one-off matter. They committed themselves to on-going expressions of thankfulness for their deliverance.

Jonah 1:17: The LORD's Salvation

While the narrative about the sailors was being rounded off, Jonah had, as it were, been left in the sea. The next section of the book (1:17-2:10) tells us how the LORD rescued the prophet and how Jonah responded. We are undoubtedly meant to be interested in what became of Jonah, but the emphasis in the narrative is on what the LORD did to save him, rather than simply on Jonah. This is true not only in what Jonah says in his prayer (2:2-9), but also in the two statements (1:17; 2:10) that bracket the prayer. We are taught that salvation comes from the LORD alone and he bestows it graciously, not because we deserve it. The LORD who is the Creator of all is the one who controls his creation, not just in a general way, but even in directing the activity of each individual part.

But the LORD provided a great fish to swallow Jonah (*verse 17*). We are not told how long Jonah was in the water after being thrown overboard, but his rescue does not seem to have been immediate, given the references to drowning in the following prayer (2:5,7). The LORD did not leave his servant to the fate that seemed to have overtaken him, but provided the means of his rescue. The word 'provide', or 'appoint' is a key term in the book. It is used again at 4:6,7,8 to convey the idea of the determinative and particular control that the LORD has over every aspect of his created realm. A related word is used in Psalm 147:4,5: 'He determines the number of the stars and calls them each by name. Great is our Lord and mighty in power; his understanding has no limit.' There is no reason to suppose that the LORD created some new, special animal to rescue Jonah. Rather he so directed one of his creatures that it was in the right place at the right time, and acted in the specific way that he required. The miracle is the exercise of power that the LORD alone can command (Psalm 103:19).

The LORD rescued Jonah by means of 'a great fish'. The Hebrew word is not specific, and the word used in Matthew 12:40 is similarly indefinite, 'a huge fish' or sea creature. Jonah presumably never saw it, except from an inside angle, and so it is difficult to see how it can be positively identified. Certain species can, of course, be ruled out because it would be impossible for a man to enter their stomachs.

The fact that **Jonah was inside the fish three days and three nights** – and survived – has proved an obstacle to many as regards the historicity of the narrative. At this point, they argue, we obviously enter the realm of fiction. Hundreds of years after Jonah a story has been made up around him to teach later generations important spiritual lessons. In the same way as with the parables of Jesus, it is argued that we are not meant to ask, *Did this really happen?* but, *What am I being taught?*

It is possible to attempt to make what happened to Jonah more plausible by gathering records of incidents in which individuals have been swallowed by fish and survived for longer or shorter periods. Such an approach generally does not achieve its objective, because in Jonah's case the problem lies deeper than the facts. The fundamental problem is an unwillingness to concede the possibility of the miraculous, of God acting in his creation and shaping its destiny. Miracle is taken to be synonymous with non-historical, non-real. Such an approach is antagonistic to the veracity and integrity of Scripture where there is no hesitation in ascribing such control to God. That is indeed one of the lessons of the book of Jonah. The LORD is the one who 'appoints' as he sees fit.

To treat the book of Jonah as a parable or fable is unsatisfactory. Unlike the parables of Jesus, there is no indication in the text that it was originally intended to be understood in this way. What is more, Jesus himself had no doubts about the historicity of Jonah and the events of this book. 'For as Jonah was three days and three nights in the belly of a huge fish, so the Son of Man will be three days and three nights in the heart of the earth' (Matt. 12:40). It is incongruous and demeaning to the significance of his work that the comparison should be with some fictional character and event. The three days and three nights are equally real for both. The phrase seems to imply three full days and nights, with the extended period involved emphasising the significance of the event. The New Testament use of the phrase, however, indicates that it may be a way of describing part of one day, the whole of the next, and into a third day, rather than seventy-two hours precisely.

Jonah was being punished for his sin. There is no doubt that his rebellion against the task assigned him by God deserved to be punished, and was worthy of death. While it is improbable that Jonah was a swimmer, he could conceivably have been rescued in some other way – clinging to a piece of driftwood, or swept ashore by some gigantic wave. But that was not what the LORD had determined. He wished Jonah's punishment to be as close as could be to that of dying without actual death. Because of this Jesus was able to draw out the parallel with his own death, involving the punishment for sin, and also the fact that after the experience there was a resurrection to come. This was to give his followers a frame of reference and hope when they came to grapple with the reality of the cross.

But it is unlikely that the incident spoke in this light to the contemporaries of Jonah. They were not in a position to say that Jonah's experience paralleled what the Messiah to come would have to undergo. That awaited the definitive interpretative word of Jesus himself. At the same time, various truths that are brought out in the incident would have been accessible to them: for instance, the heinousness of rebellion against God, death as the appropriate penalty for this, the fact that God is able to rescue from death, and that his grace and salvation are capable of offsetting even the most atrocious of sins. Indeed these were lessons that Jonah and his contemporaries were expected to learn from the prophet's experience.

It may be that an otherwise puzzling reference in Hosea's prophecy reflects on Jonah's experience. Hosea's ministry began around 755 B.C., not long after these events. 'Come, let us return to the LORD. He has torn us to pieces but he will heal us; he has injured us but he will bind up our wounds. After two days he will revive us; on the third day he will restore us, that we may live in his presence' (Hosea 6:1,2). The use of 'two' and 'third' may not originate in the gnomic language of wisdom sayings, but in what Jonah himself had experienced. What more could Israel, which like the prophet had been disobedient, hope for when afflicted for her sin, than that the LORD would extend to her the same favour he had so wonderfully shown to his prophet?

Jonah 2:1-10: The Grateful Prophet

With the sea having grown calm, the pace of the narrative relaxes also, and we have this extended account of Jonah's reaction to what happened to him. The authenticity of Jonah's prayer has often been questioned. It has not seemed to be in the right place. How could a prayer for thanksgiving be uttered before he was on land?

That would be to misinterpret the significance of the fish in a way that Jonah did not. Half-drowned though he was, he knew it was a pledge of ultimate deliverance. He had been in the water floundering, under the water about to drown. He felt himself abandoned by God. But being swallowed by the fish changed that. It did not remove all the physical difficulties he was in, but it certainly did ameliorate them – he could now breathe. He had no hesitation in recognising the hand of God at work in the miraculous provision made for him. If God in his mercy had not abandoned him, and had provided him with this measure of respite, then he could have hope for what the future had in store for him.

It was in these circumstances that we find it recorded, **From inside the fish Jonah prayed to the LORD his God** (*verse 1*). The narrator wants us to grasp that it was '*his* God' he prayed to. Although he had been acting in disobedience, his faith has once more asserted itself and directs his thought and action.

What is recorded for us in 2:2-9 is in poetry. Its many references to the Psalms reflect Jonah's knowledge of Scripture. Rather than being an artificial composition from various sources as some have suggested, it is the natural utterance of someone well-versed in Scripture. While he was meditating upon the strange providence of God that had brought him into this unusual situation, Jonah naturally employed words and phrases he had often previously heard – and no doubt used himself – but now in his affliction he finds a new 'depth' to them.

The prayer has an introduction summarising the whole experience (2:2), followed by three stanzas (2:3-4; 5-6; 7-9) each of which starts afresh from the horrendous ordeal Jonah has just undergone.

He said, "In my distress I called to the LORD, and he answered me" (*verse 2*) sets out the theme of this prayer. It recalls a previous prayer of Jonah at the time when he had been in the water, expecting imminent drowning. His call is not necessarily a reference to a shout of a drowning man. It relates to what he was thinking within himself, and expressing to the LORD. He is able to record that his prayer for help had been heard. The LORD had provided for him in his distress by sending the great fish within whose belly he now lay. God's answer is what faith confidently expects in situations of distress, and it is not disappointed (Psalms 18:6; 118:5; 120:1).

The second part of 2:2 restates the matter in similar words in the parallel manner characteristic of Hebrew poetry. **From the depths of the grave I called for help, and you listened to my cry.** The reciprocal nature of prayer and the divine response is emphasised by the similarity between the Hebrew words for 'I called for help' and 'you listened'. 'From the depths of the grave' is literally 'from the belly of Sheol' (NIV margin), the place of the departed.

The use of the phrase does not imply that Jonah actually died. Sheol is frequently used hyperbolically (Psalms 18:5; 30:3; 86:13). Here Jonah uses it to convey how he felt while struggling in the water. The dire prospect facing him was that of joining the dead. But God not only heard his cry of anguish; he responded by providing for him in his need.

In 2:3-4 Jonah recounts his experience in greater detail. **You hurled me into the deep** (*verse 3*). It is a mark of Jonah's faith that he is able to see his experience as under the determining hand of God (Psalm 39:9,10). It had been the sailors who had hurled him into the deep (1:15), but Jonah recognises that in this matter they were merely the instruments of God, doing his bidding. What has come upon him is the just punishment he deserved at the hand of God for his disobedience.

He had begun to sink **into the very heart of the seas** (the plural bringing out the boundless nature of the waters), **and the currents swirled about me; all your waves and breakers swept over me**. The last clause recalls the words of Psalm 42:7, where the figure was used in a spiritual metaphor. The experience of drowning was often used metaphorically in the Psalms (88:7; 69:1-2,14-15) and elsewhere (e.g. Lam. 3:54, 'The waters closed over my head, and I thought I was about to be cut off') to indicate a situation of great distress and impending demise. But in these other passages drowning is one of a number of metaphors employed to bring out the dire situation being experienced. It is only in the prayer of Jonah that drowning is referred to so extensively, because here of course it is not a metaphor, but relates to the real situation Jonah had been in.

I said, 'I have been banished from your sight' (*verse 4*) tells of how Jonah felt when he was struggling in the water. 'Said' covers inner speech, that is, thought, and not just what is spoken aloud. He felt permanently isolated from God (Psalm 31:22). Was not this what he had desired when he set out to go to Tarshish away from the presence of the Lord? But now he is experiencing what it is like to live without the sense of God's favour and presence, he has revised his estimate of how tolerable such a situation is. Such banishment from the presence of God is the just punishment of those who rebel against him (2 Thess. 1:9), but Christ underwent it (Mark 15:34) so that death's sting might be drawn for his people (1 Cor. 15:54-57).

In his affliction and distress he calls upon the LORD (Psalm 34:6; Hosea 5:15), which is the response of recovering faith. The words **Yet I will look again towards your holy temple** are better understood without the quotation marks of the NIV. They relate not what Jonah thought in the turmoil of his anticipated drowning, but rather on his expectation in the stomach of the fish after he had been swallowed. His distress caused his hope to increase, not to diminish. His affliction became a source of good to him as he realised that the LORD had intervened to rescue him, and that he could be confident that this meant there was a future role for him. The phrase does not signify seeing the temple as one who has travelled to it, but turning to it in prayer as the place where the LORD had specially shown his favour to his people, presencing himself with them there, accepting sacrifice, and above all answering prayer (1 Kings 8:30).

In 2:5-6 Jonah again recounts his traumatic experience and the salvation the LORD had extended to him. **The engulfing waters threatened me** (*verse 5*), or 'waters were at my throat' (NIV margin). His sensation was of one trapped and unable to breathe. **The deep** (the unfathomable ocean) **surrounded me; seaweed was wrapped around my head**. He emphasises the peril of imminent death that he had been in. He had sunk so deeply into the water that he had been trapped by the weeds on the ocean floor. Evidently some time had elapsed before the fish had swallowed him.

To the roots of the mountains I sank down (*verse 6*). The mountains were thought of as extending out under the sea. This is then a way of describing the floor of the sea. 'Sank down' is literally 'went down'. It is the last of the three downward movements in Jonah's rebellion. *Down to Joppa* (1:3), *down into the ship* (1:5), *down into the sea*. **The earth beneath barred me in for ever**. Most modern commentators take 'earth' here to be a special usage for 'underworld', with the imagery drawn from the bars used to close a city gate. The phrase would then be similar in origin to the 'gates of death' (Isa. 38:10) or 'gates of Hades' (Matt. 16:18), and would indicate that Jonah thought he had been trapped by death. Alternatively, the description may be of the rocks at the bottom of the sea trapping him in.

Again, however, Jonah is able to recount that what had seemed to be his fate was averted by the action of the LORD. **But you brought my life up from the pit, O LORD my God**. It was divine intervention alone that served to extricate Jonah from death. This reverses the downward movement of Jonah's rebellion by 'bringing up, causing to go up' that the LORD alone can supply from the 'pit', a term for the 'grave', or 'realm of the dead'.

In the third and final section of the prayer, Jonah again starts with the perilous situation he had been in: **When my life was ebbing away** (*verse 7*). It is a picture of weakness or fainting overtaking his life-force, as it turns in on itself, ready to expire. **I remembered you, LORD**, or, more literally, 'I remembered the LORD', not just in a general sort of way. This time he does not dwell on the details of his drowning experience, but rather on the response that was elicited from him. The LORD whose commands he was trying to forget was now remembered by him as the one who was able to save. **And my prayer rose to you, to your holy temple**. In a thought similar to 2:4, Jonah refers either to the Temple in Jerusalem as the place where God condescended to reveal himself, or the heavenly temple to which it corresponded.

Jonah then contrasts his experience in a time of danger with those whose religion was pagan. It may be that this reflects his recent dealings with the sailors, but more probably it comes out of the apostasy of the many in Israel who had espoused idolatry. They and Jonah had both rebelled, but the backsliders in Israel had not yet realised the folly of their conduct. **Those who cling to worthless idols forfeit the grace that could be theirs** (*verse 8*). The sense of 'the grace that could be theirs', which is one word in the original, is disputed. It could indicate the mercy they might receive from God. Others translate it as 'forsake their own Mercy' (NKJV), finding a direct reference to deity. Those within Israel who had abandoned the LORD for Baal worship, if they kept on in that, would not know the LORD's gracious help towards them. Alternatively, it might be a statement about their own loyalty, rather than the LORD's. Those who engage in idolatry no longer display the true loyalty that they should show to the covenant king.

Jonah sets himself over against a false response. **But I, with song of thanksgiving, will sacrifice to you** (*verse 9*). This is how the sailors had responded to deliverance given to them, and it was also the right way for those in Israel who experienced the LORD's blessing. But the sacrifice would not be just once. **What I have vowed I will make good**. This probably refers to on-going acts of worship; not just a thanksgiving that is offered once, but a total attitude that moulds and shapes a life. In Jonah's case it is virtually an expression of repentance and return to the LORD. The vow of future worship and obedience was what would condition his life from henceforth. The concluding **Salvation comes from the LORD** is an acknowledgement of what the LORD has done for Jonah. It implies that he alone could have done it; salvation is his prerogative. It also sets the scene for the prophet's new obedience. He has now to grapple with the full implications of this reality. This is the breath of new obedience, rather than a specific resolve. Jonah still had problems that would have to be worked out, but he now realised running away was not going to be the way to find an answer.

The narrative then reverts to prose, and simply states **And the LORD commanded the fish, and it vomited Jonah onto dry land** (*verse 10*). We do not know where, but presumably it was in Palestine. If the ship had not gone far when the storm arose, it would perhaps have been near the starting point of the voyage. Once again it is the LORD's sway that holds in the realm he has created. The mercy shown to Jonah removes his right to complain about mercy shown to others.

Jonah 3:1-4: Sent Again

The story begins all over again. This section (3:1-4) parallels the
narrative of Jonah's original commission in 1:1-3, but now the
ending is different. It is not Joppa Jonah goes to, but Nineveh as he
had been told. His obedience, however, is not yet whole-hearted,
as chapter 4 will show. But he did go.

It is a measure of God's magnanimity that we read, **Then the
word of the LORD came to Jonah a second time** (*verse 1*). The
expression used corresponds to that found in 1:1. The runaway
prophet is privileged to hear God speaking to him once more. He
has paid the penalty of his earlier disobedience and is again
enjoying fellowship with God (Luke 15:32). He is not debarred
from further service. The LORD who had saved Jonah still has a
mission he wants him to carry through.

We are not told how long elapsed between 2:10 and 3:1. It is
improbable that it happened as soon as Jonah reached the shore. He
would have been physically and emotionally drained by all that he
had gone through, and he would no doubt have been given a
suitable interval to recover. It is, however, unlikely that a lengthy
period of time was involved. The command to go to Nineveh is still,
as in 1:2, one of considerable urgency.

**"Go to the great city of Nineveh and proclaim to it the
message I give you"** (*verse 2*). 'The great city' refers primarily to
its size, but overtones of its political influence and the grandeur of
its buildings are not lacking. The magnitude of this strategic city is
again emphasised in the following verse. To it Jonah is required to
deliver the divine message and nothing else. A prophet's mission
was not one where he had liberty to say what he wanted. It was
God's message alone that his messenger may proclaim in the divine
name (1 Kings 22:14; Jer. 1:7; 23:28; John 7:16; 12:50; 2 Cor.
2:17).

Jonah obeyed the word of the LORD and went to Nineveh
(*verse 3*). What a change from last time! This is the chastened and
renewed Jonah, acting in compliance with the divine injunction. He
has considered his ways and resolved to walk in obedience, and so

he hastens to obey the divine command (Psalm 119:59,60). 'Arise! Go!' (3:2, literally), and now 'Jonah arose and went'. His actions are 'in accordance with the word of the LORD', not what he himself thought would be for the best.

Again, the narrator omits details we might want to be informed about: how long did the journey take, how did Jonah travel - by foot or by donkey, what route did he follow, what difficulties had to be overcome to get to Nineveh. About these nothing is said, because they were inessential to the story. We must therefore pay greater attention to what is added, presumably because the narrator felt this could not be missed out. **Now Nineveh was a very important city**.

The idiom employed here is literally rendered 'Nineveh was a city great to God'. The same phrase is used of Gibeon (Josh. 10:2), though it was not physically a large place. The greatness referred to would thus be of status, rather than size. That it was 'great to God' may convey the idea of a superlative, 'very important', as in the NIV translation. However, it may well go beyond that.

What is being emphasised is that the city was of significance and importance in God's sight: God cared about it. That theme will be developed later (4:11). But we need to grasp it now to understand what is going to occur.

Because it is said that 'Nineveh *was* a very important city', the conclusion has often been drawn that the city no longer existed when the book was written, otherwise it would have been 'Nineveh is a very important city'. But that need not be implied by the Hebrew usage. In looking back to the past, the narrator is emphasising what was true when Jonah was there, and is not saying anything about conditions in his own day. The phrase has no implications for the time of composition of the book.

The further description given of the city has also been obscure to translators: 'a city of going of three days'. One way of understanding it is as a description of the physical size of Nineveh. It is improbable that it meant that it took three days to travel round its circumference. No ancient city was that large. It is often suggested that the reference is not just to the city proper, but to the much larger surrounding 'metropolitan district'. That approach is backed up by what is said in Genesis 10:11 where its origins are associated with Nimrod who moved up from Babylon to build four cities, Nineveh, Rehoboth Ir, Calah, and Resen. It seems that these four cities are there collectively called 'the great city', and that might explain the use of the term here in Jonah as referring to the administrative area centred on Nineveh, but containing other towns also.

The 1978 edition of the NIV adopted another possibility: 'It took three days to go all through it.' This looked at the matter not from the angle of travelling round the perimeter of the area involved – which would have been as strange a way of describing a city's size in the ancient world as it is now – but of visiting every part of it. That fits in with the idea of Jonah moving extensively through the city, preaching at various points in it so that his message would be extensively known.

There is another way in which the phrase may be understood. The rendering now found in the NIV, **a visit required three days**, while still leaving open the previous possibility, also permits the phrase to be taken as a reference to the customs of Eastern etiquette. While Nineveh was not the capital of Assyria at this time, it was an important city in which there would be a standard procedure for receiving foreign visitors. As the Assyrians were highly superstitious, foreign visitors would cover not just political emissaries. Prophets would be accorded an equal, if not greater, status. A proper visit could not be hurried. The day of arrival would be followed by the day of formal presentation of one's message to the appropriate authorities, followed by the day of departure. What we are being told then is that Nineveh was not a small town where a visitor might begin to speak unannounced, but a royal city where the due protocol had to be followed. The significance of this is to emphasise that God's gracious warning was being extended to a truly major city.

On the first day, Jonah started into the city (*verse 4*). It is not at the outskirts of Nineveh that he proclaims the message, nor is it after one day's travel into the town. There is no mention made of the second or third day, presumably because of the immediacy of the response. He began his first day's activities, and – then we are not told precisely how far into the first day, but the implication is not too far – **he proclaimed: "Forty more days and Nineveh will be overturned".**

This is a message of impending doom. 'Overturn' is somewhat ambiguous. It can be used of all sorts of turning and change from the physical destruction of the cities of the plain (Gen. 19:21,25,29) to emotional transformation, 'My heart is changed within me' (Hosea 11:8). Here, however, in the context of a message of warning, its meaning is quite clear. What is more, the destruction is in the near, not the distant, future. Although 'forty' is found in the measurement of various critical periods in Scripture – the rain at the start of the flood (Gen. 7:12), the period of testing in the wilderness (Psalm 95:10), the temptation of Jesus (Matt. 4:2) – it seems here just to indicate a short definite period, as we might say 'a month' or 'thirty days'. What is going to happen to Nineveh is not going to be long postponed.

There are a number of interesting questions that may be explored in connection with Jonah's message.

(1) Is this all that he said? It seems unlikely. The terse style of the narrative has demonstrably led to condensation in many places (1:10; 4:2), and that seems probable here also. Certainly the knowledge the king shows of the grounds of divine condemnation in 3:8 suggests that Jonah clearly told them why this judgment was impending.

(2) Did Jonah tell them about his own experience? From the book of Jonah itself there is nothing to prove this. In the New Testament, however, Jesus clearly says, 'This is a wicked generation. It asks for a miraculous sign, but none will be given it except the sign of Jonah. For as Jonah was a sign to the Ninevites, so also will the Son of Man be to this generation' (Luke 11:29,30). There is an increasing tendency to interpret the sign of Jonah in this passage not as pointing to one who had survived drowning, but to one who came with a prophetic message from God. Jesus would

then be like Jonah in that both presented the word of God, but neither would be a miraculous sign, for no sign would be given to that generation (Mark 8:12), only the proclamation of the truth of God.

Such an understanding of Luke 11:29,30 is unsatisfactory in that it implies there are two different meanings for 'the sign of Jonah' in Jesus' teaching. Matthew 12:39,40 clearly identifies Jonah's being three days and three nights in the belly of a huge fish as constituting the sign which Jesus' own experience will parallel. This must also be the meaning intended in Matthew 16:4 and Luke 11:29,30. It is not the message that they both bring that Jesus refers to, but himself and Jonah as persons. Although 'will' in 'so also will the Son of Man be to this generation' (Luke 11:30) might be a logical future, it is more convincing to take it as a real future, referring to something that Jesus was not yet at the time of speaking, but would be thereafter. What he and Jonah had supremely in common was that both would undergo a death-experience connected with God's judgment on sin, and both would have a miraculous deliverance from death by the power of God. That would constitute the sign to be given to their generation.

It is thus the case that when Jonah preached in Nineveh, we are not to think of him as only uttering the words, 'Forty more days, and Nineveh will be overturned.' The main theme of his message was God's impending judgment on sin, so as to stir up the Ninevites to the gravity of their situation. But he also informed them about his own experience of the consequences of disobeying God, and of how God's power can save from even the most extreme circumstances. In this way we can see that the message Jonah eventually brought to Nineveh went further than that announced in 1:2. Originally the emphasis had been on divine displeasure with the conduct of the Ninevites. Now it became one of imminent punishment, but with the prophet himself as a living example of God's willingness and power to save.

Jonah 3:5-10: Nineveh's Repentance

As before (1:16), Jonah temporarily fades from the narrative, while attention is focused elsewhere. The preaching of one man is blessed by God to bring the heathen city to repentance (3:5). The impact of his proclamation is felt at the highest level in the land, and the king not only abases himself but makes public humiliation official policy (3:6-9). Such a genuine and general repentance does not go unnoticed by God, and the threatened disaster is averted (3:10).

The Popular Response (3:5). **The Ninevites believed God** (*verse 5*). A truly astonishing response! So much so that many have doubted if it actually occurred. They argue that if such a major city of the ancient world had indeed turned to the LORD, then some record of it would have survived. That is, of course, just what has happened, and the record is before us in Scripture. That there have not been found any secular records bearing on this event is not too surprising. If Jonah's mission is dated between 780 and 755 B.C., then few records have survived from that troubled period of Assyrian history. Those that have reveal many internal problems. For instance, each year from 765-759 B.C. has a note of an outbreak of plague, or of a revolt in some city of the land, or – and this would probably have seemed worst to the superstitious Assyrian mind – an eclipse of the sun.

Throughout the first half of the eighth century B.C. Assyria was threatened by powerful tribes from the north, particularly by the kingdom of Urartu, near the Caspian Sea, and her zone of influence contracted considerably. It was not a matter of dominating an empire that was the objective of public policy, but the security of the traditional Assyrian homeland itself. It may be that the upheavals and sense of impending catastrophe were influential in predisposing the Ninevites to accept Jonah's message when it was brought to them.

But what is meant by they 'believed God'? Because faith and repentance are like two sides of a single coin, answering this is linked to the question of the nature and genuineness of their repentance, as testified to in the New Testament (Matt. 12:41; Luke 11:32). If there was a widespread, deep and genuine turning to the LORD, why did this not have a substantial impact on the subsequent history of Nineveh? The troubled nature of the times may explain why there is no contemporary Assyrian record of the 'revival' at Jonah's preaching. So too would the probable suppression of any records of such an 'outlandish' aberration by subsequent generations of Assyrian scribes, who would evaluate matters from their pagan standpoint. But how could the spiritual impact of such a revival have degenerated so swiftly as to warrant Nahum's scathing indictment of Nineveh a century later? The impact of Jonah's revival would undoubtedly fade, but if it had been genuine, would not the history of Assyria from 745 B.C. on, when its fortunes were restored, have been affected by it?

To cope with these genuine difficulties, it is suggested that the faith described in 3:5 is something less than conversion to monotheism and acceptance of the faith of Israel. Elsewhere the Old Testament opens up the possibility of an awareness of God and his demands on the part of non-Israelites (Gen. 20:11; 39:9; 42:18). Nebuchadnezzar (Dan. 3:28-30) and Cyrus (2 Chron. 36:22,23) displayed such an attitude of reverence towards Yahweh, but without abandoning their polytheistic world-view. That also seems to have been the sailors' reaction in 1:16. What has happened here is more than an acceptance of the accuracy of Jonah's prediction. The Hebrew term used indicates a trust in God as the sender of the message. It may be significant that it is 'God' that is used here, and not the covenant name *Yahweh*, rendered 'the LORD' in the NIV. They accepted what Jonah was saying, and were prepared to rest in the veracity of the god – presumably they identified him as one, if not the chief, of their pantheon – on whose behalf he was speaking.

Such an interpretation may also fit 3:10 and the New Testament references to the repentance of the Ninevites. Although it is possible for an individual to humble himself before the LORD, and yet not abandon his evil ways, as seems to have been the case with Ahab (1 Kings 21:25-29), what the Ninevites experienced was real, and measured up to the amount of light accorded them. They did not ignore the warning sent to them, and so God looked with favour upon the change that took place. That is why Jesus used them to warn the Jews of his day. 'The men of Nineveh will stand up at the judgment with this generation and condemn it; for they repented at the preaching of Jonah, and now one greater than Jonah is here' (Matt. 12:41; Luke 11:32). The men of Nineveh are competent witnesses to be called on the day of judgment to testify against those who have ignored the warnings given them. Even in Jonah's day, the response of the Ninevites should have acted as a spur to the covenant nation to respond to God's warnings (see on 1:2).

That the repentance of the Ninevites, though real, did not last, is not surprising when we consider the history of the chosen people themselves. Though being privileged with far greater light, their loyalty to the Lord frequently proved ephemeral. It is not at all impossible to suppose that the passage of ten to thirty years in a pagan environment meant that the changes which had occurred in Nineveh became a thing of the past.

It is clearly pointed out that their new perception of God and of themselves profoundly altered the behaviour of the people of Nineveh. **They declared a fast, and all of them, from the greatest to the least, put on sackcloth**. The outward affliction of their bodies by abstaining from food and wearing coarse, uncomfortable garments, was associated with times of grief. Sackcloth was thick, coarse cloth, often made from goat's hair, and usually worn only by the poor (1 Kings 21:27; Neh. 9:1,2; Isa. 15:3; Dan. 9:3,4; Joel 1:13,14). They adopted an outward posture to reflect their genuine conviction on hearing Jonah's message regarding their sinfulness. It is emphasised that this reaction was not just on the part of a few, but was widespread in the city, affecting all classes of people.

The Royal Decree (3:6-9). It was therefore not surprising that news of what was happening in the city came to the palace. There would have been royal residences in the city, as it was an old one of considerable size – but in fact it is not precisely stated that the king was there. Indeed the term 'king of Nineveh' is often objected to as being an anachronism, introduced by a later writer, unfamiliar with the terminology uniformly used elsewhere, 'king of Assyria'. But two factors mitigate such a challenge. 'King of Samaria' is used on occasions in the Old Testament (1 Kings 21:1; 2 Kings 1:3) as well as the customary 'King of Israel', and here where the emphasis is on the city itself, and not the whole empire, this may have been a natural variation. Alternatively, if Jonah's visit to Nineveh occurred at some point in the period 780-755 B.C., at that time there was considerable reduction in Assyrian territory, and it may well be an accurate description of the current political realities in the reign of Ashur-dan III (773-755 B.C.).

The king shared in the general reaction. **When the news reached the king of Nineveh, he rose from his throne, took off his royal robes, covered himself with sackcloth and sat down in the dust** (*verse 6*). 'The news' may be of the reaction going on in the city, or just of the contents of Jonah's message, for prophecies regarding the welfare of the state would have been relayed to him without delay. The king too is convicted of the wrong that has been perpetrated, and humbles himself. His royal robes would have been costly and grand. Sitting on the ground is the posture of humility and self-abasement. It may also have been in the open-air for all to see.

What the people had already spontaneously initiated is now formally and officially approved by the king. **Then he issued a proclamation in Nineveh: "By the decree of the king and his nobles: Do not let any man or beast, herd or flock, taste anything; do not let them eat or drink"** (*verse 7*). The issuing of a joint decree is something that was common later on in Persian times, and may indicate that the weakness of the king at the time of Jonah's visit was such that he ruled jointly with a council of nobles. The fast is extreme being extended to include animals, both cattle and sheep. The 'them' in 'do not let them eat or drink' refers to the animals, because the word for 'eat' is literally 'pasture', or 'graze', which of course applies only to animals. Again, the evidence we have for such a custom of involving animals in times of public humiliation and mourning only comes from a later Persian period, but there is no reason to suppose that this widespread and deep-felt reaction to Jonah's proclamation could not have led to such a decree earlier on. **But let man and beast be covered with sackcloth** (*verse 8*). All are to express their sorrow and grief at the situation in which they find themselves by donning sackcloth.

The response that is enjoined upon the people goes beyond the physical. Prayer is required (cf. 1:6; 1:14; 2:2). **Let everyone call urgently on God**. The situation is so dire that they must not be half-hearted in approaching the God who has given them this warning of impending doom. Such prayer is in contrast to the situation of the sailors earlier when each called on his own deity. Moral amendment is also required. Only a radical change will make a difference. **Let them give up their evil ways and their violence**. These are the words of the king of Nineveh, not Jonah, but they seem to require that Jonah's message be more than the words of 3:4. He also told them why divine judgment was impending upon them. 'Violence' refers to any infringement of human rights and not only physical harm. Nineveh throughout its history had an altogether justified reputation for rapacious behaviour (Nahum 2:11,12; 3:19). Here it is recognised as being wrong, and they are called to turn from their evil ways.

But it is not viewed as being automatic that their repentance will lead to divine forbearance, and that their turning will induce a divine turning. Just as the pagan captain and his crew had recognised the sovereignty of divine action (1:6, 14), so too do the king and his nobles. **Who knows? God may yet relent and with compassion turn from his fierce anger so that we will not perish** (*verse 9*). The same thought is captured in Joel 2:14: 'Who knows? He may turn and have pity and leave behind a blessing.' The repentant recognise that they have no case to argue for acceptance. Their future well-being is dependent solely on divine grace. Yet, though their grounds for hope are faint, they are not totally without foundation, for why else would God have sent Jonah with his message of warning?

Divine Reprieve (3:10). The narrator then adds an authoritative comment to interpret for us what has happened. **When God saw what they did and how they turned from their evil ways, he had compassion and did not bring upon them the destruction he had threatened** (*verse 10*). There is a play on words in the original here that is often found in the Old Testament. The same word may be used to describe moral 'evil' or 'sin', and also 'calamity' and 'disaster'. Indeed the one is often the outcome of the other when God acts in judgment. So here their '*evil* ways' would have resulted in the evil of *destruction*, had not God responded graciously to the acceptance given to his message and decided to act otherwise. They proved the genuineness of their repentance by their deeds (Acts 26:20). It is not their pious actions or prayers that merit forgiveness.

These two verses (3:9,10) and also the phrase 'a God who relents from sending calamity' (4:2) present a problem as regards what is being said about God. The word the NIV translates as 'with compassion' (verse 9) and 'he had compassion' (verse 10) is in many other translations rendered by 'relent' (as the NIV does in 4:2) or 'changed his mind'. It is not only a matter of feeling sorrow or pity; it also indicates an altered determination as to how to act. Indeed, the AV used 'repent' to render this word. Now, however, repentance is only used of turning away from what is wrong and sinful, and there is no suggestion that what God had been about to do was anything other than executing just and proper judgment on the sin of Nineveh. But there is still a problem: how can it be said that God relents, or changes his mind? If we say this, are we not diminishing God by making him appear arbitrary or indecisive? Can God relent and still be the unchanging one?

The Old Testament does not hesitate to affirm both that God is unchanging, and that he can and does alter his attitude towards people and his way of dealing with them. It is interesting to find both these truths stated in the one chapter of Scripture, 1 Samuel 15. In verse 11, the LORD tells Samuel, '*I am grieved* that I have made Saul king, because he has turned away from me and has not carried out my instructions,' while a little later Samuel says to Saul, 'He who is the Glory of Israel does not lie or *change his mind*; for he is not a man, that *he should change his mind*' (1 Samuel 15:29). The words in italics all render the same basic word, which is also that found in Jonah 3:9,10; 4:2.

There is no ultimate inconsistency between the two modes of expression. When God is said to change his mind, matters are viewed from our human perspective. It appears to us that there has been a change in God, but what has in fact changed is our human conduct. Saul was no longer the man he had once been, but was persistently disobedient. The Ninevites here have also changed their conduct, but in the opposite direction, away from their evil ways. God would have been inconsistent if his attitude towards them had remained the same despite the change in their behaviour. God is consistently against sin. There is no variation in his loathing of it, or in his determination to punish it. That is a constant feature of God's character.

When God announces that his judgment is about to fall upon the sinful, it is a statement of what will inevitably happen if they continue on their present course. But it is a conditional statement. It is intended to alert the wayward and bring them to repentance. If that occurs, then God responds appropriately to the changed circumstances. 'If at any time I announce that a nation or kingdom is to be uprooted, torn down and destroyed, and if that nation I warned repents of its evil, then I will relent and not inflict on it the disaster I had planned. And if at another time I announce that a nation or kingdom is to be built up and planted, and if it does evil in my sight and does not obey me, then I will reconsider the good I had intended to do for it' (Jer. 18:7-10). Even though God in his omniscience knows that a change on the part of the nation will take place, it does not compromise his truthfulness to announce the inevitable outcome of its present course of conduct, *if persisted in*. Though it may not be explicitly stated, the announcement of impending disaster is conditioned on continuing disobedience, just as enjoyment of the blessings of God's covenant is conditioned on obedience. The just judgment of God takes into account the attitude and situation of those to whom his demands are addressed. It is only because God does respond in this way that the sinner who believes in Jesus can come to know divine acceptance.

The judgment of God is always just. Four generations had to pass before the iniquity of the Amorites reached full measure (Gen. 15:16), and the LORD brought the Israelites back into Canaan to execute his judgment on them. Nineveh too already had a black history of idolatry and oppression, but the change that took place at Jonah's preaching showed that they were not yet so spiritually blind and hard as to warrant national overthrow. Their response averted, at least temporarily, their extermination. Because they had trembled at his word and become truly contrite, God was pleased to turn aside the disaster that would otherwise have engulfed them (Isaiah 57:15; 66:2).

That such a response should result from one man's preaching in a pagan environment like Nineveh constitutes a perpetual source of encouragement whenever and wherever the gospel is preached.

Jonah 4:1-4: The Furious Prophet

Having brought the story to a conclusion as far as the Ninevites were concerned in 3:10, the narrator now turns to consider Jonah's reaction to the LORD's reprieve of Nineveh. In the structure of the book this chapter parallels chapter 2, which set out Jonah's response to the deliverance granted to him by God. But now we do not hear a song of joyful praise. Jonah did not want Nineveh reprieved and he is furious with God.

But Jonah was greatly displeased and became angry (*verse 1*). The first clause is literally, 'It was evil to Jonah a great evil,' continuing the play on the word 'evil' found in 3:10. The prophet's attitude is that the lack of calamity coming upon Nineveh was itself a calamity. He displayed the discontent of a faith that lacked understanding. His reaction is described in a very strong fashion. It goes beyond mere irritation to fury. Jonah is burning with rage -- violently angry with the way God has acted in showing compassion. In this he shows that he still did not appreciate the sovereignty of divine grace. Though he had obeyed God and gone to Nineveh, it was not as one who was completely in harmony with God. He had still a lot to learn.

Now it is easy to assess Jonah's behaviour at this point as petty, churlish and mean-minded. Indeed, his attitude is far from being commendable. But we should not write off the prophet too readily. For one thing, the LORD does not punish him, but rather treats him with patience and concern, so as to bring him to realise what is wrong. This is not the disobedient prophet, running away from his divine commission, but the perplexed prophet, obeying without understanding. Until we grasp the measure of Jonah's perplexity as to why God was so slow to act in judgment against evil and evildoers, we should not be quick to condemn him.

We notice that he acts in faith and sets out his problem before God. He is arguing with God; he is opposing what God has done; but he is not doing so by turning his back on God. **He prayed to the LORD** (*verse 2*). This is not the only place where Old Testament prophets express their difficulty in understanding what God is doing (Jer. 12:1; 15:18; 20:7).

Jonah first of all reveals what his problem had been all along. **O LORD, is this not what I said when I was still at home?** He presents it as a matter of 'my word' against the LORD's word, and he rather thinks his own was better. He does not specifically identify what he had said, but it seems to have been the case that in his own country he had expected that bringing a warning of judgment to Nineveh would result in a display of divine compassion. **That is why I was so quick to flee to Tarshish.** Jonah is concerned to justify himself and not God. His prayer is all about 'I', 'me', 'my' – six times in the NIV, nine times in the Hebrew of 4:2-3. He still thinks he was right – but right about what?

Several possible explanations of Jonah's complaint do not seem valid. It was not that he himself was going to suffer loss of face through bringing a word of judgment that did not come to pass, as if he had been a false prophet. The people's own consciences had smitten them with the truth of the accusations made against them. Nor is it necessarily the case that he saw Nineveh as the future harriers

and destroyers of his people. They had already had contact with Israel
on three occasions (see on 1:2), and they were a formidable military
power at the height of their empire. But if the historical setting of
Jonah has been rightly judged, Nineveh at this point was not a threat
to anyone, and there seems no reason to credit Jonah with a
knowledge of what the future held in terms of a revival of Assyrian
power.

There seem to be two aspects to his complaint. There was a
genuine desire to see Nineveh punished. It was all right for the LORD
to save Jonah when he was being judged for his disobedience, but
it was not right for mercy to be extended to the enemies of God's
people. The God of salvation was to confine his mercy to one
people, and not to extend it to foreigners. Jonah, though presumably aware of all the faults that could be found in Israel, did not want
to see divine blessing extended elsewhere. Instead of showing the
Ninevites favour, as he had to Jonah and Israel, God should have
punished them. Jonah could not see how God could be concerned
about any other people for their own sake.

But it was not just xenophobia. Jonah had a real problem
grasping how it was that the LORD could act in this way. He had
forgotten just how undeserving Israel itself was. God's grace had
not been extended to it on account of some merit in Israel (Deut.
7:6-8). There was no way divine compassion could be channelled
only along the routes approved or understood by human reasoning.
Ultimately divine grace towards sinners cannot be understood. It
does not have a reason. It simply reflects the way God is.

Jonah had a first rate theoretical knowledge of God. He is able
to cite a fine confession just as he had done in 1:9. His problem is
still that of living out that confession in practice. **I knew that you
are a gracious** (outside any and every covenant relation) **and
compassionate** (linked with understanding and love as a
mother to her child) **God, slow to anger and abounding in love**
(covenant loyalty), **a God who relents from sending calamity**.
This confession picks up the words of Exodus 34:6, 'the compassionate and gracious God, slow to anger, abounding in love and

faithfulness', which had played a major role in determining Israel's perception of the LORD (Exod. 32:14; Nahum 1:3; Num. 14:18; Neh. 9:17; Psalms 86:15; 103:8; 145:8; Joel 2:13). Joel 2:13 may well be the source of the last clause, 'who relents from sending calamity'. (For a discussion of 'relents', see on 3:10.) This was the very God whose compassion Jonah himself had recently experienced in being rescued from drowning. But he still did not understand. He still found fault with God for saving those he felt to be beyond the circle of redemption. He was angry with God for acting in a way that he, Jonah, did not understand or approve. At root Jonah was finding fault with God for being the way he is.

With **Now, O LORD** (*verse 3*) he turns to the substance of his petition. **Take away my life, for it is better for me to die than to live**. A similar request had been made by Elijah after he had failed to turn the land back to the LORD (1 Kings 19:4). Elijah did not expect to see results from his zeal and activity on behalf of the LORD; Jonah had. Elijah felt he was no better than his fathers. He had failed God, and desired to be taken away. Jonah is speaking out of a sense of personal affront. The LORD has failed to live up to his expectations, and he petulantly wants no more of it. Is there an element of despairing challenge? 'Once you showed Elijah there was a deeper purpose in living. Have you a similar message for me?'

But the LORD replied, "Have you any right to be angry?" (*verse 4*). 'Are you right to be angry?' A question to bring him to see the error of his position and get through to him despite his being worked up with his bad temper. 'Is your anger justly kindled?' This is a challenge to Jonah to get his thinking straight. This twice repeated question (here and in 4:9) sets out one of the major themes of the book. Has Jonah, as the representative of a people chosen by God for no merit on their part, a people favoured by God even when they go astray, as a prophet who in his disobedience has personally known the saving hand of God in his life, any valid grounds for objection if God out of his mercy shows compassion to others also? The answer is obviously that man has no right to challenge God on the way he extends his mercy.

Jonah 4:5-11: The LORD's Concern

Jonah was furious with the LORD for showing compassion to the repentant Ninevites. Once again he is at odds with God, and again we see the LORD's gentleness and compassion towards his angry prophet. The LORD seeks to cajole him into accepting the love that motivates the divine actions by providing him with an object lesson in divine sovereignty (4:5-8). He then repeats his inquiry about whether Jonah's attitude can be justified (4:9). The concluding divine speech contrasts Jonah's attitude and the LORD's, arguing from what Jonah felt towards the plant that had been provided to shade him to how God is rightly concerned about human and animal life. The narrative ends with a question. We are not told how Jonah responded. What matters is how we respond. Do we grasp the greatness of God's love? Are we eager that others enjoy it?

The Object Lesson (4:5-8). **Jonah went out and sat down at a place east of the city** (*verse 5*). It is difficult to decide when Jonah did in fact leave Nineveh. It could have been at the end of the three day period mentioned in 3:3, or later just before the forty days (3:4) had expired, or it might even have been after the completion of the forty days. A solution depends on our conclusion as regards when it would have been obvious that the judgment he had warned of had been averted by the repentance of the Ninevites. The statement of 3:10 is the narrator's inspired comment upon what happened, and in the light of his technique of finishing one matter before proceeding to the next even if that disrupts the temporal sequence, it is difficult to draw any conclusions from it as regards the order of events.

The most plausible scenario seems to be that when it was obvious that there was widespread repentance among the people, Jonah realised that this would lead to the exercise of divine compassion. He then uttered the words of 4:1-4 in the city probably not long after the end of the three days. He subsequently went outside to wait and see what would happen, and during that period the LORD challenged him. This makes sense of a number of features of the terse narrative. The picture of him waiting for judgment to fall even after the forty days have elapsed is far-fetched. That he is found 'at a place east of the city' fits in with him having gone through it from the west over a short period of time.

There he made himself a shelter, sat in its shade. The hot climate would have made waiting in the open an uncomfortable experience. To shade himself from the sun, Jonah made a makeshift shelter. Wood is a scarce commodity in Mesopotamia, and it would probably have been with stones or mud bricks that Jonah constructed the shelter. At best a few bits of shrub might have been used for the roof. The area would not have been uninhabited and it would have been easy for him to get food and water from local people.

Jonah **waited to see what would happen to the city** may not imply that he doubted the genuineness of the repentance of Nineveh. There were instances where punishment followed, even though there had been repentance, most notably in the death of David's child even after he had confessed his sin in connection with Bathsheba (2 Sam. 12:13-18). If the Ninevites were placing their hopes in a 'Who knows?', so too could Jonah. Despite the contrition of Nineveh, God might not disappoint him and might still bring destruction upon them.

It was not just Jonah's attitude towards Nineveh that was uncomfortable. Even with his shelter, it would have been far from pleasant out under the sun. **Then the LORD God provided a vine and made it grow up over Jonah to give shade for his head to ease his discomfort** (*verse 6*). The name used 'LORD God' is unusual. Although found in Genesis 2-4, it is not frequent elsewhere, and seems here to mark a deliberate change from LORD to God. LORD is the covenant name of God who has acted in mercy towards his people. This is particularly shown by his compassionate treatment of Jonah despite his fuming and reluctance to accept what God has done. The use of 'God' here and in 4:7-9 points to his action as the supreme ruler of all. He provides (see on 4:7) as he sees fit and as he alone can.

The plant provided is similar to the 'great fish' of 1:17. There is no necessity for supposing that either were newly created species. Although we do not know the precise type of fish or plant, the lesson being taught is God's control over all that he has created. Perhaps the plant was a gourd or a vine. Although several species are known to be fast growers, this one sprouted at an unprecedented rate. Its broad leaves would have provided shelter in the sweltering eastern heat, making a more effective roof for the structure than any Jonah had been able to construct. **And Jonah was very happy about the vine**. The LORD's action brought him relief in his situation, alleviating its discomfort. Perhaps it also caused Jonah to think that his self-appointed surveillance of the city would bear fruit after all. Had the LORD come round to his prophet's way of thinking? Was this a token of divine approval of what he was doing?

But at dawn the next day (*verse 7*), after only one day in which Jonah enjoyed the benefits given to him by the shade of the plant, **God**, the Creator, the one with power to act over what he has made, **provided a worm**. 'Provide' is the same word that is used in 1:17 of the fish, in 4:6 of the vine, in 4:7 of the worm, and in 4:8 of the wind. God exercises a comprehensive and effective control. Be it a small worm, or a large fish, they are directed as he sees fit. Now, however, the purpose behind it is not relief, but destruction. **Which chewed the vine so that it withered**. The miracle is again to be found in the control exercised over creation. The plant does not wither in some unnatural way, but through divine oversight of a natural phenomenon. It happens precisely when and how God has determined.

When the sun rose, God provided a scorching east wind, and the sun blazed on Jonah's head so that he grew faint (*verse 8*). Again God's control is seen in that the situation in which Jonah finds himself is aggravated by the divinely summoned scorching wind. This dry, hot wind which withers green growth, and causes considerable physical distress, is a well-known phenomenon in the area – but it is under God's control and serves his purpose. Jonah at once feels the effect of the plant's death, and begins to suffer from sunstroke. **He wanted to die, and said, "It would be better for me to die than to live."** The words are identical to 'It is better for me to die than live' (4:4). If the provision of the plant had eased Jonah's lot and his bad temper somewhat, the situation was now reversed.

He was back into his old mood again, and wishing he were dead. He speaks on the basis of common humanity, and challenges God's right to destroy.

The Repeated Inquiry (4:9). In a repetition of what happened in 4:3, **But God said to Jonah, "Do you have a right to be angry about the vine?"** (*verse 9*). Again the words are identical, 'Have you any right to be angry?' This repetition emphasises the link between the two sections of the chapter and prepares the way for the inferences that are drawn. Jonah's anger is now focused on the loss of the vine, and what has happened to it. **"I do," he said. "I am angry enough to die."** He felt he was being victimised by what had happened to him. Jonah was sure he was right in what he considered should have happened to Nineveh. Not only was God wrong in what he had done to the city, but also in what he had done to the prophet.

The Challenging Question (4:10-11). It is the LORD who speaks, reflecting a change in emphasis from the Sovereign who has in his control all he has created, to the covenant God who deals in mercy with his people. He remonstrates with Jonah and seeks to bring him to see the folly and small-mindedness of his position. **But the LORD said, "You have been concerned about this vine, though you did not tend it or make it grow. It sprang up overnight and died overnight"** (*verse 10*). 'Concern' is a feeling which goes out towards one in trouble. It is often translated 'pity', but is more than a sympathy, because it moves on into action taken to assist the other party. It reflects the attitude of the Messianic king towards the weak and the poor (Psalm 72:13), though the word is used most often in a negative context, such as the divine pronouncement, 'I will allow no pity or mercy or compassion to keep me from destroying them' (Jer. 13:14). Concern would have led to sparing them, as here.

Jonah was concerned about a mere plant, that had come and gone. He had not had to take any trouble to grow it or tend it, but now that it is dead, he is so stirred up that he would have been prepared to go to great lengths to preserve it. If Jonah felt in such a way about a plant, then how can he be critical of God's attitude towards Nineveh? The force of the argument is from the lesser to the greater, and the intensity of Jonah's reaction is being employed as a lever to give him insight into the LORD's attitude. If he is unwilling to accept this insight, he will be in a self-contradictory position.

But Nineveh has more than a hundred and twenty thousand people who cannot tell their right hand from their left (*verse 11*). To justify his concern, the LORD points out the size and significance of Nineveh (see on 1:2; 3:3). Usually the 120,000 are taken to be children, leading to estimates of the total population around 600,000. Archaeology suggests that figure may be on the high side for the city, though not if the surrounding district is included. It is possible that those 'who cannot tell their right hand from their left' is an idiomatic expression, not for some early stage of human development, but for lack of ability to discriminate between courses of action. The figure of 120,000 would then be for the total population ('people') of the city, who are described as being unable to reach a considered and informed decision.

Nowhere does Scripture suggest that being outside Israel deprives people of knowledge of right and wrong. They are untaught, and while this does not make them innocent, it provides grounds for dealing with them gently. The addition **and many cattle as well** is probably not due to some Eastern pre-occupation with cattle as a source of wealth, but rather relates to Jonah's attitude towards the plant. If the plight of the Ninevites does not arouse him, perhaps the prophet who was concerned about the plant, would show concern about the animals that would be lost if a Sodom and Gomorrah style conflagration engulfed the city. It is urging Jonah to review his scale of priorities.

We are not told about how Jonah responded, for it is the reality of the LORD's compassion that is the dominant theme. **Should I not be concerned about that great city?** Although the question comes first in the verse in the Hebrew, the NIV puts it last to prevent what can sound like an anti-climax to us by ending the book with 'cattle'. The reader of the book of Jonah in every generation is being left with a testing question to grapple with. How do we perceive the grace of God? Does the example of the concern of 'God our Saviour, who wants all men to be saved and to come to a knowledge of the truth' (1 Tim. 2:3-4) provide the pattern for our concern?

Study Guide

These study questions are designed to assist individual reflection on the significance of Jonah for today. They may also provide useful starting points for those leading discussion groups. The Biblical references indicate passages of Scripture of relevance to each topic, but we may not always have a complete or final answer to what is asked.

Jonah 1:1-3

verse 2: What role should patriotism play in the Christian's behaviour? (Romans 9:1-5; 10:1; Galatians 3:28; 6:10)

Are unbelievers used by God today to stir up the church to renewed obedience? (Matthew 5:46,47; 1 Corinthians 5:1; 6:6)

verse 3: What does Scripture teach about God's presence and knowledge? (Psalm 139:7-12; Jeremiah 23:23,24; Hebrews 4:13)

Do these divine attributes have the same significance for the believer and the unbeliever? (Job 34:21,22; Psalms 11:4,5; 17:3)

Jonah 1:4-6

verse 4: Is seeing God as the one who controls the elements and the weather an outmoded way of perceiving things? (Job 36:26-33; 38:22-30; Psalm 147:8, 15-18; Matthew 5:45; Acts 14:17)

verse 5: If 'perfect love drives out fear' (1 John 4:18; Romans 8:15), how can 'fear' be used to describe a proper Christian attitude? (2 Corinthians 5:11; Philippians 2:12; 1 Peter 1:17; 2:17; Revelation 14:7; 19:5)

verse 6: Under what circumstances does God not answer prayer? (Proverbs 1:23-28; Isaiah 1:10-15; 59:1,2; Jeremiah 11:9-11; 14:10-12; Zechariah 7:8-14; James 4:3)

Jonah 1:7-10

verse 7: Are there circumstances where the use of lots might still be legitimate? (Acts 1:26)

What conditions would have to be satisfied before such a procedure is used? (1 Corinthians 10:31; Ephesians 4:1,29; Colossians 3:17) *verse 9*: When may a confession of faith be correct and orthodox, and yet be sadly deficient? (Isaiah 29:13; Ezekiel 33:31; Matthew 15:8; Mark 7:6; Acts 8:13-21; James 2:14-26)

When we realise we have sinned, what should we do? (Leviticus 26:40; Psalm 32:5; Proverbs 28:13; 1 John 1:9-2:1)

Jonah 1:11-16

verse 14: What responsibilities do we have regarding the preservation of life? (Genesis 9:6; Exodus 21:12-14; Mark 8:2,3; Acts 27:10,11, 31-36)

How may we reconcile our knowledge of human actions with Scripture's teaching regarding God's sovereign control over events on earth? (Psalms 75:6-7; 115:3; Daniel 4:17,25,35; 1 Corinthians 1:28; Philippians 2:12-13)

verse 16: What considerations should be taken into account in making vows, that is, promising to God to do something, or to follow some particular course of conduct in future? (Proverbs 20:25; Ecclesiastes 5:4-6; Acts 5:4; 18:18; 21:23)

Jonah 1:17

verse 17: Why did God perform miracles? (Exodus 4:2-9; Matthew 11:2-5; John 11:40-42; 20:30-31; Romans 15:18,19)

What parallels exist between Jonah's experience and Christ's? (Matthew 12:39-41)

Jonah 2:1-10

verse 1: What part does recognising our relationship with God play in returning to him? (Luke 15:18)

Have there been times when Scripture has 'come alive' for you in a special way?

verses 4 and 7: What is the Christian experience corresponding to looking towards the temple? (Hebrews 4:14-16)

verse 9: What place should thanksgiving have in our lives? (Luke 17:16; Ephesians 5:4,20; Colossians 2:7; Hebrews 13:15)

Jonah 3:1-4

verse 1: 'The LORD disciplines those he loves' (Proverbs 3:12).
What should we learn from this? (Job 5:17,18; Psalm 119:67;
Hebrews 12:4-13; James 1:12; Revelation 3:19)

How are we to use renewed opportunities for service? (2
Chronicles 33:10-16; Isaiah 1:16-19; Matthew 21:28-32)

verse 4: What word of warning has the church to bring to the
world today? (John 16:8-11; Acts 2:30; 3:19; 17:30; 26:20; 2
Timothy 2:25-26)

Jonah 3:5-10

verses 5 and 6: Are outward religious acts valid on their own?
(Isaiah 58; Joel 2:12,13; Matthew 6:16-18)

Should fasting have a role in the life of New Testament
believers? (Mark 2:18-20; Acts 13:3; 14:23)

verse 10: Is God inconsistent when it is said that he 'relents'?
(Jeremiah 18:7-10; 31:18-20; Ezekiel 18:27-32; 33:12-20; Luke
15:20)

Jonah 4:1-4

verse 1: How should we react when favour is shown to others?
(Luke 15:25-32)

verse 3: What should we do when we find ourselves out of step
with God? (Psalm 119:11,18,34; Proverbs 3:5)

verse 4: Are we ever right to be angry? (Exodus 32:19; Mark
3:5; Ephesians 4:26-27, 31; James 1:19-20)

Jonah 4:5-11

verse 6: How should we react to the blessings God bestows?
(Psalm 103:2,10; Isaiah 63:7; Luke 17:18; Ephesians 5:20; 1
Thessalonians 5:18)

verse 11: Can we set bounds to God's love? (Isaiah 45:22;
Ezekiel 18:23; John 3:16; 1 Timothy 2:3,4; Titus 2:11; 2 Peter 3:9)

Micah

Overview

A prophet – and a 'minor' one at that – writing in the closing years of the eighth century B.C. may at first appear a remote and distant figure. How can what he said then possibly be relevant to us today? But as we study Micah's prophecy, we become quickly aware of uncomfortable parallels between his situation and ours.

Western civilisation has abandoned its Christian foundations. In Micah's day, Judah had abandoned its religious heritage. There was indeed an outward willingness to worship the LORD (6:6,7), but Micah anticipates our Lord's test in Matthew 12:33-35, and examines the fruit present in society – and there is little to commend it. Violence was used to seize property (2:2) and to waylay passers-by (2:8). Justice was perverted (3:9). Commercial trickery and deceit were prevalent (6:10-12). Family life was distorted (7:5,6). Micah exposes the moral and social evils that prevailed in his day, and traces them to their source. The religious spokesmen of his day no longer spoke the truth (2:11; 3:11). Pagan practices had become prevalent (5:12-14).

It is the reality of the LORD's judgment upon all this that Micah brings out. He uses the example of Samaria, the capital of the Northern Kingdom, Israel, and its fate as a warning to Jerusalem and Judah (1:5-9). He is unsparing in his denunciation of those who are misusing their power in the land (2:1; 3:2-3, 9-10). He speaks as one who knows what the outcome of their behaviour inevitably will be, but yet he speaks in the hope that his words of warning will serve to turn them from disaster, as in measure they did (see comments on 3:14).

But though judgment was postponed by repentance, Micah knew that it would only be for a while, and that the people of Judah would revert to their old ways. The LORD would chastise his people for their rebellious ways, and yet his judgment would not be his final verdict on them. Three times Micah presents the future hope for a remnant who will be preserved by divine grace. On the first occasion, it is only a brief glimpse of this deliverance that we have (2:12,13). The second time, in chapters 4 and 5, it takes on a clearer outline, and we are introduced to the Ruler from Bethlehem, through whom the LORD will accomplish his people's deliverance. The third expression of hope closes chapter 7, and is designed to lead us to exclaim 'Who is like the LORD?', as Micah declares his faith in the one who will be true to his covenant commitment and redeem his people despite their unworthiness.

Micah 1:1: Introductions are important

When we read Micah, or one of the other prophets, we are often so eager to get to the 'real message' later on in the book that we pass over the introduction quite quickly. But we should not be in such a hurry. When Micah was writing down the message, he had already been preaching for quite a number of years. He was guided by the Holy Spirit to put this title at the beginning of his book, and it gives us four important starting points to help us appreciate and understand what follows.

(1) *The Divine Message.* The first thing the title tells us is that this is **the word of the LORD**. The prophets often employ this phrase, especially in the titles or superscriptions of their works (Jer. 1:2; Hosea 1:1; Jonah 1:1), to describe what is being said. But the fact that it is frequently used should not blind us to the astonishing claim that is involved in it. The message that follows is not to be attributed to the insight of human genius. It is rather a word **that came**. This message was revealed by divine initiative. Micah does not ask for any credit for having thought it up. What he claims is that it is **the vision he saw** (Isa. 1:1; Nahum 1:1). Here he uses a word that may refer not just to a vision, but also to a message perceived in other ways, for example, by hearing. But it was a message given to Micah, and he then in his preaching and writing relayed the information that had been entrusted to him by the LORD. This name when in small capital stands for Jehovah, or Yahweh, the personal name of the covenant God of Israel. He was speaking to his people, and Micah was the herald proclaiming the message of the sovereign king.

(2) *The Divine Messenger.* The title also identifies for us the individual who received God's word, **Micah of Moresheth**. The name Micah was a very common one, and means 'Who is like the LORD?' In this or a longer form, Micaiah, it is used of fourteen men in the Old Testament. After Micah, perhaps the best known of them is another prophet, who lived more than a hundred years earlier (1 Kings 22; 2 Chron. 18).

We would have expected Micah to introduce himself in the usual way by telling us who his father was. Instead he tells us that he came from the Judean country town of Moresheth. It is most probably the same place as Moresheth Gath, mentioned in 1:14, which lay south west of Jerusalem, about halfway to the Mediterranean Sea (see Map II). Since Micah would not have been known in his hometown as Micah of Moresheth, we may deduce that he became used to introducing himself in this way as he went to other parts of the country during his prophetic ministry. Much of it was probably in Jerusalem, where he was certainly well remembered a hundred years later (Jer. 26:17-19). This passage also indicates that Micah's message, if not Micah himself, was known to King Hezekiah (715-686 B.C.), and his ministry (no doubt along with that of his better known contemporary, Isaiah) played a role in the reformation that occurred under Hezekiah. Micah was thus one whose ministry was blessed in his own day, and was remembered much later on.

We know no more about Micah and his personal background than this. Sometimes he records his thoughts and personal feelings for us. But he does not tell us how or when God called him to be a prophet, or precisely when and where he delivered his various messages, or any of the other information we might have liked to know about him. We are not to be taken up with his personal circumstances. What matters is that he is the one through whom the LORD spoke, and still speaks.

(3) *A Time of Crisis.* The title does, however, tell us that it was **during the reigns of Jotham, Ahaz and Hezekiah, kings of Judah**, that Micah received his message. This is vital information for us. It enables us to locate Micah's message historically, as we have indeed already begun to do. In this way we can better understand what God was saying through his prophetic herald to the people of his own day. But, more importantly, when we see similar circumstances occurring today, it allows us to work out what God's message is for us. He does not change. His attitude to

man's behaviour and his remedy for man's situation have always been the same. It is therefore not only legitimate but also necessary for each generation to apply the word of the LORD to its own time. In that way our perception of what is happening around us will be improved, and it may be that we will respond in time to the warnings that God's word still conveys to us.

The reigns of Jotham (750-731 B.C.), Ahaz (735-715) and Hezekiah (715-686) of Judah were years which saw the collapse of the political strength that had been built up earlier in the century both in the northern kingdom of Israel under Jeroboam II (793-753) and in the southern kingdom of Judah under Uzziah (792-740). During their reigns the weakness of surrounding nations and their own friendly attitude towards each other had permitted them to extend the territory of their kingdoms so that together they ruled over almost all that David and Solomon had once controlled at the peak of Israel's influence. But by Micah's day there had been a considerable change in the international situation. The energetic and very competent Tiglath-Pileser III (745-727) had come to the throne of Assyria. The northern kingdom had been weakened by internal dissension after Jeroboam's death, and came increasingly under Assyrian control, culminating in the destruction of the capital city, Samaria, in 722 B.C. after an unsuccessful rebellion.

Judah was spared the same fate because Ahaz had been following a pro-Assyrian policy and was willing to pay substantial tribute. Although Hezekiah was out of sympathy with his father's policy, for the first part of his reign he made no open moves to break Judah's status as a tributary state. He did, however, try to tackle the internal problems of his kingdom.

But it was not just a period of political tension and upheaval that Micah lived through. There was also an economic and social revolution. The heyday of Uzziah had brought much wealth into the land, but it was not evenly distributed. The rich got richer, and invested their wealth in land, undermining the traditional pattern of rural life, and creating many social problems. As they selfishly pursued their own interests, they thought nothing of exploiting the poorer classes. There was also an erosion of standards in the religious life of the nation. Idolatry was openly fostered by Ahaz, and even those who claimed to worship the LORD became satisfied with the external aspects of worship without a true heart engagement. Prophets, priest and rulers condoned the prevalent materialism and religious superficiality. Micah was commissioned by the LORD to expose these conditions and to call for a return in the life of the nation to the standards of behaviour towards one's neighbour which God's covenant had laid down.

(4) *The Two Capitals.* The final piece of information conveyed in the introductory title is that Micah's message was **concerning Samaria and Jerusalem**. Mentioning the capital cities rather than the kingdoms of Israel and Judah is unusual, and perhaps reflects Micah's perception as a countryman that the declining standards in the nation had spread from the centre outwards. Although his message was for all the inhabitants of the land, it was addressed in a special way to those in positions of influence, and particularly in the capital. Although he begins by recording an early message about Samaria, most of the book focuses on the south. By the time Micah came to write down his message Samaria had already fallen, but its fate served as an example for Jerusalem and Judah in Hezekiah's day. Indeed, through the messages sent to these two capital cities and their nations long ago, God still addresses us and warns us about our behaviour and responsibilities. An outward show of religious activity does not satisfy him, if it is not matched with a true concern for all the requirements of his word (Matt. 7:21-23). Those whom the King invites to enjoy the inheritance he has procured for them are those whose allegiance to him has been practically expressed in their actions towards the citizens of his kingdom (Matt. 25:34-40). Micah's message is concerned with the application of these principles of God-honouring living.

Micah 1:2-7: Where Judgment Begins ...

Micah starts the record of his prophetic ministry by going back over the earliest messages he had received from God. He returns to the closing years of the reign of Jotham, the king of Judah who died in 731 B.C. This was before the northern kingdom of Israel had been wiped out by the Assyrians, who captured its capital city of Samaria in 722/21 B.C. But it was already a time when the Assyrians were making their presence felt in Syria and Palestine (2 Kings 15:29).

Micah is, however, looking behind the human actors on the international political scene. They were only doing what God had ordained should occur. Micah has been shown how the hand of God, the judge of all the earth, will work. He is concerned to emphasise the reality of God's judgment, both on the nations (1:2) and on God's chosen people (1:5-7). Micah wants to puncture the complacency of those who feel they have a secure relationship with God, but who in reality are living as rebels against him. Unless they mend their ways, they will be the first to experience God's wrath.

Micah's message begins with the summons **Hear** (*verse 2*). The summons is repeated at 3:1 and 6:1, and serves to indicate the three main divisions of the book. The prophet is acting as a court-usher requiring all interested parties to pay attention to the actions of **the Sovereign LORD** as he comes in judgment. Three truths are emphasised.

(1) The LORD is not just a god of one people. He is Lord of all. **Peoples, all of you**, and **earth, and all who are in it** are his rightful subjects who should listen to him and obey (Psalm 49:1). The title Adonai is used twice (once translated 'Sovereign' by the NIV, and once as 'the Lord') to emphasise the universal dominion of the LORD, Israel's God. He is not a local deity, such as the heathen imagine, but one whose sway extends to every individual on earth, whether or not they are prepared to acknowledge him.

(2) There is also a warning conveyed to those who would suppose that God is distant, and so call into question the reality of his knowledge of what is on earth, and of his desire to intervene in judgment. He is described as **the Lord from his holy temple**. This

combines his transcendence and his immanence. The 'holy temple' refers to his heavenly dwelling place, as in Psalm 11:4 and Habakkuk 2:20 (compare also Jonah 2:7). But he is not just introspectively absorbed in the praises of the seraphim. He observes and examines what people are doing, and 'from' serves notice that in his own good time he will openly and decisively intervene in the affairs of earth.

(3) The summons issued here is so that he **may witness against you**. Now at first this may seem awkward because the rest of the chapter describes judgment against Samaria and Jerusalem, not the other nations of the world. But Micah will later return to the theme that the destiny of all nations is inextricably linked with that of Israel and Judah (4:1-4; 5:7-9; 7:10), and that God will judge the nations (5:15; 7:16,17). Now they are being called on to watch and learn. This is what will ultimately be held against them. If judgment begins with the house of God (1 Peter 4:17,18), then are those who do not acknowledge the Sovereign LORD going to be exempt? What is going to befall God's people is not some arbitrary and inexplicable act, but part of the total reality of divine judgment, which will sweep away all that opposes him.

The next two verses (1:3,4) describe the impending arrival of God in judgment using the language of theophany, as is found elsewhere (e.g. Judg. 5:4,5; Psalms 18:7-15; 68:7,8; Isa. 64:1,2). Attention is demanded. **Look! The LORD is coming from his dwelling place** (*verse 3*), that is, his holy temple mentioned in 1:2, and **he comes down**. This probably implies that his action is going to be based on close examination of the evidence (Gen. 11:5; 18:21). **The high places of the earth** may just be part of the general picture. As God descends from heaven, the first place he comes into contact with is the mountain tops (Amos 4:13). However, 'high places' were frequently thought of in ancient times as places of security from the enemy (Psalm 61:2; Obad. 3). Now in a reversal of human expectations, they are the first to experience God's presence in judgment. Also, 'the high places' were the sites of the Canaanite worship of Baal. When the LORD **treads** on them and destroys them, he exposes the impotence of the pagan deities whose shrines were there.

The presence of God affects all the earth from the highest mountains to the depths of the valleys. We are probably to take the first and third lines of 1:4 together, and the second and the fourth. The picture is one where **the mountains melt beneath him** ... **like wax before the fire** (Psalms 68:2; 97:5; Nahum 1:5; Hab. 3:6) and **the valleys split apart... like water running down a slope**, as when a violent rainstorm washes all before it down the valley. This is a graphic description of the tremendous forces unleashed when the LORD comes to judge the earth. Nothing escapes the impact of his presence. The awesome reality will be completely realised only on the final day (2 Peter 3:10), but it is anticipated in every prior intervention of God in judgment in the affairs of men.

One aspect of this situation as it affected Micah's original audience in Jerusalem must be noticed. They had been used to hearing of God going forth to rescue them and judge their enemies (e.g. Judg. 5:4,5; Psalm 68). Micah's message would not then have struck them at first as being one of condemnation for them, but rather one of encouragement: was this not God intervening on their behalf as he had done of old? But Micah is using a technique also found in Psalm 50 and Amos 1 and 2 to communicate with a spiritually complacent nation, who are sure of themselves and unaware of the breakdown in their relationship with God. He speaks at first in terms that are familiar and comfortably remote. It seems as if God's anger is directed elsewhere, then he says, 'It's you I am talking about! Not them!' In this way Micah seeks to puncture their self-satisfaction and overcome the defences they have erected against criticism.

The true focus of the prophet's message need not even have become obvious at the beginning of 1:5, when it is said that **all this is because of Jacob's transgression, because of the sins of the house of Israel** (*verse 5*). 'Jacob' and 'Israel' were descriptions involving some ambiguity. They were originally religious terms rather than political, and referred to the whole covenant people. But after the division of the kingdom at the end of Solomon's reign, Israel also became the designation of the northern kingdom. Jacob also was used as a poetic equivalent for the north (Isa. 9:8; Amos 6:8; 7:2) as well as for the whole covenant people. It would be easy for those in Jerusalem to have supposed that Micah was talking about the sin of their northern neighbours. 'Transgression' or rebellion refers to positive acts that are contrary to the LORD's requirements and in defiance of his authority. The connotation of 'sins' is more negative, indicating rather failure, default, not matching up to the standards of God's law. The religious degeneracy of the northern kingdom and its consequences are clearly spelled out in 2 Kings 17:1-23.

Micah then asks questions to trace these faults back to their source. **What is Jacob's transgression**? Literally it is 'Who is Jacob's transgression?' Sin never exists apart from sinners and Micah's question is as much about the identity of those involved as it is about the nature of their misdemeanours. His rhetorical question **Is it not Samaria**? emphatically locates those responsible as being in the capital city. It is from the attitudes of those in government and in the ruling classes of Samaria that evil influences have spread through the land. Those who should have been nourishing the life of the nation have instead been poisoning it. Next Micah turns to probe the state of the south. We might have thought he would ask, 'What is Judah's sin?' But perhaps in another attempt to startle the complacent into thinking about their situation he introduces an unexpected question. He identifies their sin by saying, **What is Judah's high place**? A 'high place' was a Canaanite sacred site, originally on a mountain top, as being in some way nearer to the gods, but later on an artificial elevation on lower ground. **Is it not Jerusalem**? Micah is implying that if you go up to Jerusalem what you will find there is not the true temple of the LORD, but, just as in Samaria, something that has been distorted and debased through the influences of Canaanite worship, and amounts to nothing more than a pagan shrine. Even though Jotham was one who did what was right in the sight of the LORD, he, like many pious kings before him, had been unable to remove the high places (2 Kings 15:34,35). Later under Ahaz, things were to become much worse, with child sacrifice (2 Kings 16:3) and the erection of a pagan altar in the temple (2 Kings 16:10-16). One of the reforms of Hezekiah's reign was to remove the high places (2 Kings 18:4).

To this point Micah himself has been speaking of what he has seen and knows about as the LORD's prophet. But now he moves on to declare the LORD's verdict against his rebellious people, and does so by citing the LORD's own words. It is not on Jerusalem that judgment is first pronounced. The North had led the way in abandoning the LORD, and it will be the first to experience God's wrath.

Therefore (*verse 6*) makes it evident that the overthrow of Samaria is not arbitrary, but the fully justified consequence of her misbehaviour. Consequently the LORD declares, **I will make Samaria a heap of rubble**. The picture is not just of a mound of stones, recognisably once a city, but rather of 'a heap of the field' (AV). It will be so obliterated that it will become just like the heap of stones a farmer gathers out of his way in a corner neglected, uncared for, unnoticed. Samaria was situated in good country for growing vines, and that is what the site will again become, **a place for planting vineyards. I will pour her stones into the valley and lay bare her foundations**. It had been 'set on the head of a fertile valley' (Isa. 28:1,4), and its demolition will involve the stones of its buildings being tossed down the slope till the site is levelled.

But it will not just be that the houses and city walls will be destroyed. It is significant that the aspect of Samaria's fall that is particularly singled out for comment is that **all her** stone **idols will be broken to pieces** (*verse 7*). They were the reason for the LORD's devastating judgment. **All her temple gifts will be burned with fire; I will destroy all her images**. Whatever adorned Samaria's temples will be burned.

Since she gathered her gifts from the wages of prostitutes, as the wages of prostitutes they will again be used. 'Prostitution' is probably best taken to refer to idolatrous worship (as in e.g. Exod.

34:15; Deut. 31:16). The precious articles that adorned the temples of Samaria had been gifts from those who engaged in false worship there. When the city is overthrown, these treasures will be carried off by the enemy to adorn the temples of their own gods.

It is worth noticing that Micah here clearly exposes the flaw in Samaria as being religious corruption and idolatry. Micah is often, and not without reason, cited as a prophet of the poor, standing out against the social injustices of his day. But this initial message directed principally at the northern kingdom shows us clearly that he understood evil practices to be outward evidence of the inner corruption of a heart estranged from God. Oppression and injustice are the symptoms of a much deeper spiritual malaise, for it is out of what is stored up within them that men speak and act (Matt. 12:35).

Micah 1:8-16: ... And Where It Ends

When others are struck by disaster, our feelings of relief at not being personally involved frequently prevent us from learning the lessons the tragedy could teach us. Micah is determined that Judah should learn from the experience of Samaria. He records his own reaction of grief and distress to the calamity about to overtake the northern section of God's people to induce his hearers in the south to be affected in the same way (1:8,9). He then goes on to tell of calamity encircling Jerusalem itself (1:10-16). The South had no reason to expect immunity from the LORD's judgment. As he had already indicated at the end of 1:5, they too were involved in practices similar to those in the North. So Micah seeks to press home the example of Samaria as a warning to the people of the South. (This was also done by his prophetic contemporary Isaiah, compare Isa. 10:11.) As we shall see, Micah emphasises the danger they are in by returning three times to focus on Jerusalem, at the end of each of the three parts of this section, in 1:9, 12, and 16.

In the previous section (1:6,7) it had been the LORD himself who spoke, but now Micah records his own reaction to the situation of which he has been informed. **Because of this** (*verse 8*) refers back to the message of judgment he has just delivered about Samaria, and its implications for Jerusalem. He therefore says, **I will weep and wail**. These words refer to the dirges and laments of the mourning rites that were customary at eastern funerals, where no restraint was placed on open expression of grief and sorrow. So devastated is Micah by the judgment which he knows is surely coming on Samaria, that he already presents himself as a mourner at the funeral of the Northern Kingdom.

To **go about barefoot and naked** were also open signs of distress, as when David ascended the Mount of Olives weeping and barefoot as an expression of his grief (2 Sam. 15:30). 'Naked' here, and on other occasions in Scripture, probably means not wearing the usual outer garments. Micah's actions seem just to have been those of a mourner, and not a pictorial representation of one going into captivity, as is the case in Isaiah 20:2.

He also says, **I will howl like a jackal and moan like an owl**, or more probably an ostrich. Ostriches were then found in the wilderness areas of the Near East and were often hunted. The reference here is to their harsh, doleful cry. The long drawn out nocturnal howl of a jackal is well known. These two animals are also linked together in Job 30:29 in a context of mourning and affliction.

In this, Micah shows himself to be like the other prophets of the LORD. They were never detached commentators on the social and religious scene of their day. Even though they had solemn warnings to deliver to unrepentant sinners, they did not let this harden their love for the people to whom they spoke. Isaiah 22:4 records how the prophet did not wish to be consoled when he considered the destruction the LORD would bring upon his people. Jeremiah in particular is not afraid to reveal the intensity of his grief over the people's sin (e.g. Jer. 8:21; 9:1). So too Micah here. It is still the case that those who present the warnings of the gospel to an unrepentant generation must do so lovingly and not harshly.

Micah makes clear that there are two reasons for his grief: the situation in Samaria, and the situation in Judah. He says for her, that is, Samaria's, **wound is incurable** (*verse 9*). There are two views about what constituted the 'wound' of Samaria.

(1) Some take it as the sin and rebellion that had struck a mortal blow at Samaria's national life. Micah is also overwhelmed with grief 'for' (not translated in the NIV) **it has come to Judah**. The same rebellious attitude against the LORD had already spread south to Judah, and not just in a marginal way. **It has reached the very gate of my people, even to Jerusalem itself**. The area immediately inside the city gate was the centre of the community where people met, the market was held, and the elders administered justice. So Jerusalem the centre of the life of the kingdom had been corrupted, and the situation in the south was desperate.

(2) In the light of 1:13, however, it may be preferable to understand the reference to Samaria's wound to be that caused by the LORD's punishment of his rebellious people. Then what Micah describes is the spread to the South of judgment such as the North had already experienced. The rendering of the NIV footnote 'He has reached the very gate of my people' presents a similar picture: the Assyrian king with his armies, acting as the instruments of the LORD's judgment, enter Judah and besiege the capital. In the years following the fall of Samaria they did make a number of incursions into Judah, culminating in 701 B.C. when Sennacherib overran the area and Jerusalem barely escaped (2 Kings 18:13-16). Micah would then be speaking of Jerusalem as 'the gate of my people', the heart of the southern kingdom, reached but not overrun by the enemy.

Micah was not himself from the capital but from one of the smaller towns of Judah. Although critical of much that went on in Jerusalem, he does not let that blind him to the repercussions that will affect the whole land if the capital falls. He speaks with intense personal involvement and concern. He talks of the whole population as 'my people'. Neither his personal origins nor his loyalty to the LORD prevent him from identifying with them. What happens to them involves him, and already their condition was causing him grief.

In the next section (1:10-12) the theme of mourning continues to dominate. Micah cites words from David's lament over Saul and Jonathan (2 Sam. 1:20), **Tell it not in Gath** (*verse 10*). The site of Philistine Gath – the name itself is common, meaning 'wine-press' – is not yet identified, and it is uncertain if it still existed in Micah's day. The saying had, however, probably become a proverb, implying that the enemies of God should not be given the opportunity to vaunt themselves over a calamity that had struck Israel. Indeed the command, **Weep not at all**, seems to imply that the disaster Micah sees coming will be so great that there will not be the time or opportunity for shedding tears.

The footnotes of the NIV, however, alert us to a feature of this passage: Micah repeatedly plays on the meanings of the names of the towns he mentions and on similarly sounded words in Hebrew. Perhaps it was suggested to him by the similarity in sound that exists between 'Gath' and the Hebrew word for 'tell'. It is not of course usually possible to convey this in an English translation. Even if it could be done successfully, this sort of literary technique is alien to us, and it is very doubtful if the effect on us would be to reinforce the solemnity of the message as it would have done for Micah's audience.

On the basis of the Septuagint, the ancient Greek translation of the Old Testament, there is another NIV footnote to 1:10, suggesting that instead of 'Weep not at all' there was originally one of these word-plays between a place name 'Acco' and the Hebrew word for 'weep'. 'Weep not in Acco' would then have substantially the same meaning as 'Tell it not in Gath', that is, a warning against carrying their weeping into the Phoenician city of Acco, which lay north of Mount Carmel (see Map II). But it is very difficult to see why Acco would have been chosen as a typical foreign city. At least Gath was mentioned in the proverb, and was also situated very close to the other towns Micah mentions. This alternative is therefore not very likely.

Micah now goes on to mention a number of other towns or possibly villages. Many of their names occur only here in the Old

Testament, though they would undoubtedly be known to the people of Jerusalem Micah was addressing. So far as we can tell they were located in the Shephelah, the fertile low foothills on the edge of the Mediterranean coastal plain, which was where his hometown of Moresheth was (see Map II). Although Micah is now describing the disaster that will come upon Judah, he still makes it somewhat distant from Jerusalem, so that the impact of the end of 1:12 is intensified. Micah seems to have selected these particular places because of the opportunity their names gave for word association that would fit his message. They do not seem to occur in any particular order, and their haphazard listing may perhaps have added to the picture of confusion he is describing.

At the end of 1:10 Micah mentions **Beth Ophrah** (or, Bethleaphrah). Its location is unknown, but it seems unlikely that it was the same place as Ophrah in Benjamin near Bethel (Josh. 18:23; 1 Sam. 13:17). The name means 'house of dust', and so in the picture of disaster, its inhabitants are commanded to **roll in the dust**, a way of displaying extreme anguish (Josh. 7:6; Job 16:15; Ezek. 27:30).

Shaphir (*verse 11*) is of uncertain location, possibly south-east of the Philistine city of Ashdod. Its name means 'pleasant' or 'beautiful', but its inhabitants are to undergo a reversal of what such a name involves as they **pass on in nakedness and shame** (Isa. 20:4; 47:2,3; Nahum 3:5). They are being led off as slaves, stripped of their clothes and exposed to their captors' taunts.

Zaanan, the next place mentioned, may perhaps be the same as Zenan (Josh. 15:37), in which case it was located somewhere near Lachish. Its name sounds like the Hebrew word for 'come out', but again the situation is reversed. **Those who live in Zaanan will not come out**. We are not certain why. Are they to be besieged? or, Are they to experience a loss of nerve and be unwilling to come out to fight? or, Is it that they will be captured and slaughtered so that they are unable to come out and escape? At any rate, their fortunes will belie the name of their town.

It is even less certain what is being said at the end of 1:11 about

Beth Ezel, which means 'house of nearness', and which has been tentatively located south-west of Hebron. Perhaps its name implies that it is a helper, or a place of refuge, but **Beth Ezel is in mourning**. Its cries of lamentation bear witness that it too is going to be engulfed in the disaster, and so **its protection is taken from you**, presumably from the inhabitants of the land who might have sought refuge there.

Maroth is yet another site that has not been located, but its name means 'bitterness', and so, unlike the last three places, it will in the impending disaster experience a fate corresponding to its name. **Those who live in Maroth writhe in pain, waiting for relief** (*verse 12*) which will not come.

The reason why there is no relief is that the **disaster has come from the LORD**. Literally, it has 'come down', and in that there is a reference back to the LORD's own coming down in 1:3. What is happening is no accident. It is the judicial intervention of their covenant LORD whom they have spurned, and consequently there can be no relief. The invading forces through whom the LORD will punish his people have reached **even to the gate of Jerusalem**. It may mean that the city itself will be under siege and so unable to help others. This in fact happened during Hezekiah's reign, when in 701 B.C. he and his army were trapped in Jerusalem by the Assyrian forces of Sennacherib – 'like a bird in a cage' as the Assyrian annals relate. In this second mention of Jerusalem (see also 1:9), Micah is emphasising that, just as the centre of national life had become spiritually corrupt, so the threat of divine retribution looms over it too.

In the third section of this lament (1:13-16) Micah again plays upon the names of places in the Judean foothills. Lachish had for centuries been a major fortress town. It lay about 48 kilometres (30 miles) southwest of Jerusalem, and therefore close to Micah's hometown of Moresheth. Lachish is similar in sound to the Hebrew word for a 'team' of war horses used to pull a chariot. But the command **You who live in Lachish, harness the team to the chariot** (*verse 13*) seems ironic. Its purpose is not fighting, but escape. It is uncertain how Lachish was **the beginning of sin to the Daughter of Zion**, a poetic reference to the population of Jerusalem (see on 4:8). We do not know of any major pagan shrine at Lachish. The **transgressions of Israel were found in you** may refer to their abandoning the LORD as their source of confidence and instead seeking security through political alliances and military strength, with which Lachish was of course very much associated. It was this secular outlook on life that Isaiah challenged in King Ahaz. 'If you do not stand firm in your faith, you will not stand at all' (Isa. 7:9; see also 2 Kings 16:5-9).

Therefore (*verse 14*), as a consequence of this pinning her hopes in the wrong place, when her military strength has failed her, Lachish **will give parting gifts to Moresheth Gath**, the fuller name of Micah's hometown, 10 kilometres (6 miles) northeast of Lachish. Moresheth sounds like the Hebrew word for 'betrothed', but the gift Micah envisages is not the dowry customarily paid by the bride's father to the bridegroom. It is rather tribute paid by the land to the conqueror (2 Kings 16:8; 18:14-16) as he deports the inhabitants of Moresheth to a distant land . **The town of Aczib** was only a few miles from Moresheth, and in the coming tragedy it **will prove deceptive to the kings of Israel**, living up to the meaning of its name, 'deceptive'. It will not give the help it had promised to the royal house. Since Aczib was in the south, Israel must refer to the covenant people as a whole. The help expected would have been to the kings of Judah, not those of the north.

Mareshah was another important fortress town, lying between Aczib and Lachish. It is related in sound to the Hebrew word for 'inheritance' or 'possession', often one taken by conquest, and so Micah again brings out part of what will be involved in God's coming judgment by saying, **I will bring a conqueror against you who live in Mareshah** (*verse 15*). The 'conqueror' would be the Assyrians (Isa. 7:17; 10:5,6). The 'I' here is undoubtedly God, and indicates that though Micah has not set out this passage as direct divine speech, there can be no doubt that what he is relating has been revealed to him by God. So close did the prophets feel

themselves to be to God, and so much did they associate all that
they had to say with what had been revealed to them, that they often
did not formally mark the transition from what was their description of the message or vision given to them and what was direct
divine speech (1:6).

Then, as an indication that he is coming to the end of this
section, Micah picks up a theme he had used at the beginning of it
in 1:10, by again looking back to David's day. It was to the cave of
Adullam that those who were in debt or discontented with Saul's
rule had gathered (1 Sam. 22:1-2). Now **he who is the glory of
Israel will come to Adullam**, another fortress town in Micah's
home territory, east of Aczib. Again, 'Israel' here is not a reference
to the Northern Kingdom, but to the covenant nation, whose glory
may have been the king, or more probably the nobility of the land
as a group. The nation's fortunes will be so strikingly reversed that
it will be the highest in the land who have to tread the malcontents'
path as they seek refuge in Adullam.

Then, for the third time, Micah focuses on Jerusalem, in effect
resuming from 1:13 the personification of the city as Daughter of
Zion. He addresses the city as a woman whom he urges to go into
deep mourning for the loss of her children. **Shave your heads in
mourning** (*verse 16*). Despite the injunction of Deuteronomy 14:1
against shaving the front of their heads for the dead in the manner
of the Canaanites, the plucking out or shaving off of hair seems to
have remained a common expression of deep anguish over the loss
of close relatives (Isa. 22:12; Jer. 7:29; 16:6). Here Jerusalem is to
mourn **for the children in whom you delight**, with more than a
hint that they had been doted over. **Make yourselves as bald as the
vulture** is a clear reference to the pale, down-covered head of the
griffon vulture. Notice that the people of Jerusalem are being urged
by Micah to engage in this mourning immediately, not in the day
when disaster strikes. He presented himself to them as a mourner,
and they were urged to join him. If they accepted Micah's word as
being truly from God, they would become as sure as he was that the
calamity of judgment would ensue. **For they will go from you into**

exile was one aspect of the curse of the broken covenant, which had long since been announced (Deut. 28:41) and would soon be fulfilled (2 Kings 17:6). If the people accepted the reality of their sin, then they would have acknowledged the righteousness of God's threatened judgment, and that would have been the first step on the pathway to restoration.

Micah has set before his people the inevitable outcome of their rebellion against God. Out of an intense and compassionate concern for the good of his fellow countrymen, such as Paul also would display (Rom. 9:1-3; 10:1), Micah has been pleading with them in tears to recognise the gravity of their situation. An evident and genuine sympathy for the plight of those addressed is still necessary in the presentation of the gospel.

But this section does not simply instruct us to consider the warnings addressed to us by others. We are also to pay attention to what is happening to those around us. Jerusalem had been shown what would happen to the towns and villages around her. Though Micah has so far only prophesied of the disaster as coming to the gates of Jerusalem, that was not to be misinterpreted. There were no exceptions then or now. The message is still the same, 'Unless you repent, you too will all perish' (Luke 13:5).

Micah 2:1-11: The Fitting Punishment

So far Micah has been concerned with piercing the complacency of his audience in Jerusalem – by making them see that they are the ones who are under threat from the LORD's judgment. Though that judgment will come upon them through enemy invasion, it will not just be the outcome of forces at work on the international political scene. The LORD determines the destiny of the nations, and he does so with particular reference to the situation of his own covenant people. The primary reason for the catastrophe that was to come on them was not political weakness, but their disobedience against the LORD. The nation had no respect for God and this had shown itself in its abandonment of his standards for living.

Micah points the finger at those who have been the chief beneficiaries of the new wealth that had come into the country with the economic recovery under Uzziah. In 2:1-5 he castigates their behaviour and announces God's condemnation of it. Then in 2:6-11 he lets us overhear a conversation between himself and other prophets who were condoning the current situation and providing a cover of religious respectability for it.

Woe! (*verse 1*) is a cry of grief originally used at funerals, but often employed by the prophets as a threatening introduction (Nahum 3:1). Micah does not point directly to those he is speaking about, or name them. He rather describes them, and lets those whom the cap fits wear it. His description also makes clear that divine punishment is not arbitrary or capricious. He clearly spells out the reasons for God's intervention against **those who plan iniquity**. 'Iniquity' frequently refers to the abuse of power so as to cause trouble and thus bring harm on one's fellows. It was no sudden temptation they had given in to. Their behaviour was deliberate and sustained. They **plot evil on their beds**, where as often in Scripture (Psalms 4:4; 36:4; 63:6) they are pictured as apart from the hustle of everyday life and alone with their thoughts. But this is no time of pious meditation for them. These people are so intent on amassing wealth that they spend sleepless nights devising schemes to satisfy their desires (Prov. 4:16), and then **at morning's light they carry it out**. They are so eager to carry out their plans that they can hardly wait for daylight to come (Hosea 7:6). What is more, **it is in their power to do it**. Wealth had flowed into the land in the days of Uzziah, but it had been concentrated in the hands of a few, and they were using it for their own selfish ends. They were in positions of influence, where they ensured that no obstacle was allowed to stand in their way.

The newly rich had more money than they could immediately spend. About the only investment opportunity that then existed was in real estate, in fields and houses. **They covet fields and seize them, and houses, and take them** (*verse 2*). Isaiah, who was a contemporary of Micah, talked about those who added house to house, and joined field to field till there was no space left for anyone else (Isa. 5:8). The smallholders of Israel were being bought out or evicted. The rich used violence to acquire property from those who would not sell to them. They were utterly unscrupulous in achieving what they wanted to the extent that **they defraud a man of his home**. As a countryman, Micah had witnessed the enormous social problems caused by the loss of the traditional small family farm and the creation of these large estates. The social structure of Judah was becoming increasingly polarised by the growing number of rootless, dispossessed farmers.

But Micah was not just concerned that the gap between the rich and the poor was widening, and about the cruelty and injustice that had attended it. He saw it as fundamentally a religious problem. The condition of society reflected an alienation in heart from God. Micah says, 'They covet', deliberately using the language of the tenth commandment (Exod. 20:17). Their outward actions sprang from an inward disregard for God's law. He also speaks of their defrauding **a fellowman of his inheritance**. The people of Israel had been taught by Moses that the land belonged to the LORD and he had entrusted it to them in their tribes and families. It was not to be permanently transferred to others (Lev. 25:23). Naboth's attitude toward his vineyard was a clear example of fidelity towards this covenant requirement (1 Kings 21). But now there was a whole class of oppressive Ahabs, trampling upon all the statutes that the LORD had laid down for his people.

Therefore, the LORD says (*verse 3*) introduces the divine word of judgment on such a situation. One problem that affects our interpretation of these verses is the identity of **this people**, or 'this family'. The word is used in Amos 3:1 to refer to the whole nation, and it may be taken in the same way here, so the ridicule of 2:4 is uttered against all Judah. But, more probably, 'this people' is the class of rich oppressors. God's treatment of them is going to match their own behaviour. To offset their plans (2:1), God says, **I am planning**. They plotted 'evil' in 2:1, and so now God plans **disaster**. It is in Hebrew the same word, which can refer to calamity or to moral evil. This word play is frequently used by the prophets to show that the calamities the LORD brings on his erring people are not arbitrary, but in response to their wrongdoing. The disaster **from which you cannot save yourselves** will be like a yoke put on an animal's neck so that it could pull a plough or a cart. No matter how the animal twisted and struggled it could not rid itself of the yoke. In the same way they will be unable to escape the coming punishment. **You will no longer walk proudly**. 'Walk' embraces every aspect of their conduct. Their total life-style has been characterised by pride towards God and their neighbours. God's judgment measures up to their offence and brings their haughtiness to an end. **It will be a time of calamity**, using the same word as is translated 'disaster' earlier in the verse. The same principle still applies. 'Do not be deceived: God cannot be mocked. A man reaps what he sows' (Gal. 6:7).

In that day (*verse 4*) when the disaster God is planning comes, unspecified **men will ridicule you; they will taunt you with this mournful song**. A similar situation is described in Habakkuk 2:6, but perhaps here the singing of a song of lamentation is in deliberate contrast to what had previously prevailed. **We are utterly ruined; my people's possession is divided up**. It may be that these words had been first sung to describe the situation of those dispossessed by the rich and powerful. **He takes it from me! He assigns our fields to traitors**. The form of the word rendered 'traitors' makes it unlikely that it refers to foreign enemies. Rather it describes those from within the covenant community who had violated God's requirements. Now in the day of God's intervention in judgment against the land, the prosperity of the landowners is reversed. Those who sang first of themselves now turn the words in bitter derision against those who had oppressed them.

Micah then addresses a further explanation to the rich as a group. **Therefore you will have no one in the assembly of the LORD to divide the land by lot** (*verse 5*). When Israel occupied Canaan, the land was divided between tribes by lot (Josh. 18:8-10). Micah looks forward to the day when God will convene the sacred assembly of the people for the purpose of redistributing the land. Those who have violated his covenant requirements will then have no representative or descendant in the assembly of the people. Because of their sin the LORD will no longer recognise them as his, and they will have no portion in the restored land.

In the next section (2:6-11) Micah shows that the rich oppressors were not isolated in the community. They had their supporters. Micah spoke as a prophet of the LORD, but there were others who also claimed to be prophets speaking in the name of the LORD. They, however, presented a different message.

It is not the usual words for 'prophesy' and 'prophet' that are to be found in 2:6,11. Probably the word used here could have ambivalent overtones, not unlike the use of 'preach' in English, as in 'Don't preach at me.' The false prophets wanted to silence Micah and those who agreed with him (their command is addressed to more than one person), and so, **"Do not prophesy," their prophets say. "Do not prophesy about these things"** (*verse 6*). Micah's message was too critical of the influential groups on whom they depended for their livelihood for them to be comfortable. Similar opposition to prophetic warnings are recorded elsewhere (Isa. 30:10; Amos 2:12; 7:10-13). The other prophets were sure **disgrace will not overtake us** (compare 3:11). They were relying on the fact that they were God's covenant people, but without realising that such status required obedient covenant living. The message of the prophets of affluence accepted and reinforced the prevailing optimism that there would be no end to their prosperity, for God would remain with them, no matter what.

It is difficult to be certain who is speaking in 2:7. Some take the first part of the verse to continue the words of the false prophets as they recall the covenant blessings of the house of Jacob and emphasise the goodness of God's promises. 'Such things' as the disaster and judgment Micah was prophesying could not possibly come from their God. Their theology seems to have arisen from a partial acceptance of divine revelation, grasping the promises but de-emphasising the obedience that the LORD required and would reward (Deut. 5:32,33). The NIV, however, presents the first part of 2:7 as Micah's own words. He is trying to prick the conscience of the covenant people, and so says to them, **Should it be said, O house of Jacob: "Is the Spirit of the LORD angry? Does he do such things?"** (*verse 7*). God does not wish to be angry with his people and to utter threats against them because of their misconduct. That is not how he wants to act towards his people. There ought to be no need for such things to be said, nor would there be talk about God's anger and judgment if only his people's loyalty towards him went beyond lip-service and involved a real commitment to the life-style his covenant demanded of them.

The use of 'my' in 'my words', referring to the LORD, indicates that a divine address begins in the second part of 2:7, and it continues to the end of this section. **Do not my words do good to him whose ways are upright?** Since what the covenant LORD says to his people tells them how to behave, it ought to be a source of good, bringing blessing to those who uprightly observe what is required. But that has not been the case with Judah. **Lately my people have risen up like an enemy** (*verse 8*). Within their own land they have acted like marauding troops returning from battle. The only thought on their mind was to pillage and plunder. **You strip off the rich robe from those who pass by without a care**. Unsuspecting travellers have fallen foul of their desire to snatch all that they can.

Their despicable behaviour has extended to women and children also, quite contrary to covenant statutes, Exodus 22:22-24 (also Deut. 27:19). **You drive the women of my people from their pleasant homes** (*verse 9*). This picks up a theme that was mentioned in 2:2 also. The action of the oppressors was destroying the fabric of family life in the land, and not just the current generation. **You take away my blessing from their children for ever**. 'My blessing', or 'my glory', may refer to God's majestic deeds on behalf of his people, and probably here points specifically to the portion of his land allotted to each family and intended to be handed down from one generation to the next. The rich are grabbing this land and so preventing the children from enjoying a privilege that should have been theirs.

The commands that are found next are addressed not only to the rich oppressors but also to their sympathisers, those who have condoned and joined in their covenant violations. They thought they were providing additional security for themselves as they built up their grand estates. But the certain verdict of God's judgment comes to them in the words **Get up, go away!** (*verse 10*). The victors are themselves divinely evicted. **This is not your resting place**. Canaan had been given to God's people as a place of physical rest, and also as the place where they could enjoy fellowship with him (Deut. 12:9; Psalm 95:11; Heb. 4:8,9). But though the land had been ideally suited to their needs, now **it is defiled, it is ruined, beyond all remedy** by their breaches of covenant, and so they will not be permitted to remain in it. They had broken the covenant, and so they were not permitted to remain in possession of the blessings of the covenant (Deut. 30:18; Josh. 23:15-16).

In 2:11, Micah returns to the theme of 2:6 – the false prophet. This technique of reverting to a previous theme has already been used in 1:15, looking back to 1:10, to indicate the end of a section of a speech or writing, and to a certain extent it prepared Micah's hearers for a change of subject in 2:12. The LORD presents a hypothetical, but not impossible, set of circumstances. **If a liar and deceiver comes and says** (*verse 11*). The false prophet is described as a 'liar', literally one 'walking with/in wind and falsehood'. There is no substance to what he says, and so he is a 'deceiver'. But when such a person comes and presents a picture of material prosperity and indulgence (Isa. 56:12), **I will prophesy for you plenty of wine and beer**, then **he would be just the prophet for this people**! God no longer calls them 'my people', but stands apart from them. They would readily acclaim such a person as a true prophet. Those who give people a pleasant message that fits in with what they want to hear are always given a ready reception (Jer 5:31).

This section stands as a permanent indictment of the misuse of wealth. Scripture does not condemn material blessings, but it recognises very clearly the dangers that ensue when the 'love of money' comes to dominate a life (1 Tim. 6:10). James, in the New Testament, criticises just as strongly as Micah the way in which the rich abuse their economic power to oppress others (James 5:1-6). This need not be just a matter of individual conduct. When we live in a land of relative affluence, we must consider how it is that we behave towards communities and nations that are less prosperous. The temptation to pursue a course of action which is to our advantage just because we have the power and economic muscle to do it (2:2) must always be resisted. Might does not make right. Rather 'do not withhold good from those who deserve it, when it is in your power to act' (Prov. 3:27). The rich – the individual and also the community – are to do good, to be generous and willing to share (1 Tim. 6:18).

We must also watch how it is that we form our opinion of ourselves. There are always those who will flatter the rich. 'Men praise you when you prosper' (Psalm 49:18), and especially if they think some of that prosperity might come their own way. It is only in the light of the searching standards of God's word that we may truly assess our conduct. We must take care that our lives are not spent just storing up things for ourselves, without considering where we stand in relation to God (Luke 12:21,34).

Micah 2:12-13: The LORD At Their Head

There is now a sudden switch in the theme of Micah's message, from judgment to hope. There are other passages in the Old Testament, such as Psalm 13:5 and Hosea 1:10, where hope suddenly brightens a previously dark scene, but it seems improbable that Micah would have relayed these words to the people of Jerusalem immediately after the message of condemnation that precedes them in the text. That would have been to endorse the approach of the prophets who were opposing him, for they promised peace and security from the LORD no matter how the people behaved.

It will not do, however, to argue that 3:1 is the natural continuation of 2:11, and that therefore these two verses have been misplaced. The problem is solved when we recognise that this is not the order in which Micah proclaimed his message in Jerusalem probably in the earlier years of Hezekiah's reign, around 710 B.C. Rather the order is a feature of the way he later wrote up the substance of his prophetic ministry, perhaps in the aftermath of Sennacherib's invasion of 701 B.C. Each of the three main sections of his prophecy (chapters 1-2, 3-5, and 6-7) were similarly structured: first exposure of sin, then judgment, and after that restoration and blessing. This arrangement underscored that while judgment would undoubtedly come from the LORD upon his erring people, it was never going to be his last word on their destiny. Before 701 B.C., Micah had given such encouragement to those in Judah who were loyal to the LORD, and who were perplexed as to what would follow the devastation foreshadowed in chapter 1 or the threatenings of 2:10. Later, in writing up his message, he continued the same theme, because he realised that though conditions had temporarily improved, the repentance professed by Judah was superficial. There still lay ahead an even more severe time of judgment through which the faith of those who were the LORD's would have to be sustained. We too may learn from this bright glimpse of the salvation of God to look beyond whatever darkens the immediate prospects of God's people to the time 'when the day dawns and the morning star rises' (2 Peter 1:19).

The details of the passage have proved difficult to interpret even for those who accept that they are found in the right place. Some, following the lead of Luther and Calvin, have considered that the transition from judgment to blessing is too sharp to be allowed, and have argued instead that what is presented here is the LORD gathering his people to lead them into judgment. But this does not easily fit in with the picture at the end of 2:13 'the LORD at their head'. The tone at that point is one of victory rather than of impending punishment.

But if this is a scene of deliverance, where and when is it to be located? There seem to be two main possibilities. (1) A case may be made for interpreting it as coming after the situation envisaged in 2:10 has arisen, with the people led off into exile. These verses would then refer to the return of the Jews from Babylon. There is, however, a difficulty with this, because in that case 2:12 and 2:13 would seem to be in the wrong order. If 2:13 is a picture of the people breaking out from the imprisonment of Babylon, it should surely come before the picture of security that is presented in 2:12? It is certainly improbable that Babylon itself would be presented in 2:12 as a pen and a pasture for the people of God during the exile. Indeed Babylon does not seem to have featured up to this point in Micah's message.

(2) There is much to be said for another interpretation which views 2:12-13 against the background of the threatened invasion with which chapter 1 had ended. That invasion would sweep through Judah, but though the Assyrians wreaked havoc and captured many important towns in the land, Jerusalem did not fall (2 Kings 18,19). Chapter 1 had ended with the land invaded, and Jerusalem with a noose around its neck. In this section Micah foretold to those who put their trust in the LORD that he would provide safety for them. Because that deliverance has many features in common with the other gracious acts of the LORD on behalf of his own, there are many parallels that may be traced.

The dominant note of 2:12 is that of certainty: no longer the certainty of the LORD's judgment, but of his deliverance. **I will surely gather. I will surely bring together**. The promises of God are not vague aspirations, but settled and reliable. The situation is one where the people have been scattered, possibly in terror before the advancing enemy army, and the divine Shepherd is going to round up his dispersed flock. The theme of gathering is taken up again at 4:6,7.

I will bring them together like sheep in a pen, like a flock in its pasture. His care of them will be complete, extending to security in the pen and nourishment in the pasture. Jerusalem became this place of security in Sennacherib's invasion.

The three sections of the prophecy that focus on the hope that Micah brought to the people share the theme of the Shepherd. It is found again in the description of the LORD's deliverer in 5:4, 'He will stand and shepherd his flock in the strength of the LORD, in the majesty of the name of the LORD his God', and also in the prayer of 7:14, 'Shepherd your people with your staff, the flock of your inheritance.' The links that Micah himself introduces in chapter 5 between the shepherding and the Messiah make it natural to see in the deliverance the LORD provided for his people at that time a foreshadowing of the deliverance he provides through the Good Shepherd of the Sheep (John 10:11).

There are two descriptions given of the people who are gathered – **all of you, O Jacob** and **the remnant of Israel**. These are alternative identifications of the same group, occurring in parallel lines of the text. 'Jacob' is a reference to the true covenant people. The principle Paul states of 'not all who are descended from Israel are Israel' (Rom. 9:6) applies here. It is not physical descent that counts but spiritual. The promise that the divine Shepherd will ensure that none of his flock is missing (John 10:27-29) refers to those who are loyal in heart to the LORD, and whose living evidences that loyalty. Those whose behaviour reveals their alienation in heart from God (2:1-11) are excluded.

'Remnant' is a two-sided word. In the first instance it speaks of disaster and loss ahead. Israel as a people will not emerge unscathed from the scrutiny and outpouring of divine judgment. But there is promise in it too. It will not be a total catastrophe, for there will be a divinely preserved remnant. It will consist of 'all', and the picture is of the vast number involved in that 'all'. **The place will throng with people**. The picture moves from sheep to people. The place (Jerusalem) will hum with noise because so many people will find protection within its walls.

There is another presentation of the LORD as his people's deliverer in 2:13 – not now as the Shepherd, but as the Breaker. We no longer hear the LORD himself speaking. The quotation marks of the NIV are misplaced, and should come at the end of 2:12, not 2:13. This is now the voice of the prophet, not relaying the LORD's words, but speaking about him and presenting for us another future scene he has been permitted to see. It is a different picture. The vision of the shepherd and the sheep had already faded by the end of 2:12.

Now we are presented with a view of the people hemmed in by their enemies in Jerusalem. But the day of liberation from their confinement has arrived. The **one who breaks open the way** has arrived. In this too we have a picture of Christ, though one that I don't think is found in these precise terms elsewhere. What he does is described by a word that could be used for breaking down the wall of a captured city (2 Kings 14:13). It was also used of divine anger breaking out against those who have offended God (Exod. 19:22). It can also mean to urge someone to a particular course of action (1 Sam. 28:23). It is a word which speaks of power that sweeps all obstacles before it, effectively undermining and demolishing all that would resist it. It is a presentation of the LORD as a warrior overthrowing his enemies (Isa. 42:13; Jer. 9:16-19).

But the picture is not that of a liberator who comes from outside to release those who are confined within some prison. The movement both of the liberator and the liberated in this verse is from within outwards. Not only is freedom provided for them by another, but it is by one who has been with them, who has identified with them, and who has shared in their lot (Heb. 2:14).

Mention is made of **the gate**, and this recalls the two previous occurrences of this word in 1:9 and more especially in 1:12, both referring to Jerusalem. We notice that **they will break through the gate and go out** because the breaker, the liberator, had done so first of all. Their deliverance is only possible because he **will go up before them** through the gap made in the encircling enemy lines and provide the path they follow. He is the captain of their salvation (the 'Pioneer of their salvation', Heb. 2:10, *Amplified Bible*; Heb. 6:20), and he is trail-blazing the path his people have to follow. As Hosea had prophesied, the rescue extended to Judah did not depend on human effort, but came from the LORD himself (Hosea 1:7; Isa. 37:36).

The liberator, the one who breaks through the barriers and obstacles for them, is also **their king** who **will pass through**

before them. We then see in the words **the LORD at their head** that merging which occurs also in Micah 5, where the one who will be ruler over Israel stands and shepherds his flock in the strength of the LORD. If it is not identification – and it may well be that – it certainly shows God's approval of him, something that the kings of Judah they had known had frequently lacked. Here is the king in whom the ideal of kingship would be realised, and of whom the LORD would so approve that he is prepared to identify with him and his actions. In that it is fitting to see a foreshadowing of Christ and his ministry.

Micah 3:1-12: Exploitation Denounced

Micah 3-5 constitutes the second portion of the prophecy, marked as the others are by an initial summons to hear. This section follows the same general pattern as the first: exposure of evil, the LORD's condemnation of those involved, and then a message of hope and deliverance. But this time Micah alters the proportions of these themes, and says much more about the coming deliverance in chapters 4 and 5. Chapter 3, however, focuses on what was wrong in Judah in Micah's day.

Micah exposes the malpractice, motivated by greed, of three main groups in the land – rulers, prophets, priests – before going on to oppose their theology and overturn it. In 3:1-4 and also 3:9 he forthrightly presents his critique of the rulers for their perverse motivation (3:2,9), unsparing brutality (3:2-3,10), and greed (3:11). The focus is on the false prophets in 3:5,11. The inevitability of the LORD's judgment on all this is found in 3:12. In 3:8, in passing, Micah gives an impassioned statement of how it was that he came to act as a prophet.

The first section of the chapter covers 3:1-4. **Then I said** (*verse 1*) has caused considerable perplexity to commentators. Ordinarily it would form part of a conversation, but no background is given. Some have suggested it is to be understood as a continuation from 2:11. Micah is telling us what his preaching was in contrast to that of the false prophets. But it is not necessary to take 2:12-13 as intruding into an original block of material. The words may simply be resumptive, and could well indicate the major role that Micah himself played in producing the book that bears his name in the form we now have it.

Listen calls for attention. The summons is repeated, 'Hear this!' in 3:9. (The original words are the same on both occasions.) **You leaders of Jacob, you rulers of the house of Israel** both refer to the Southern Kingdom. Samaria had by this time been captured, and Micah uses the pair of names, Jacob and Israel, to address his hearers in Judah in their capacity as the surviving representatives of the people of God. Their nation was not just a political entity, but a people who derived their existence and constitution from the LORD himself. The description points to the basis of the following denunciation of their behaviour. They were not upholding the standards the LORD expected to be maintained by his covenant people.

The 'leaders' had originally been heads of households and tribes who sat in judgment in disputes, but by this time the reference is probably to the court officials in Jerusalem. The 'rulers' were literally the 'deciders' – a reference perhaps not only to the judiciary but also to the civil administration. The charge is put to them, **Should you not know justice?** That was what would be expected of the officials in the capital (Deut. 1:16,17; 16:18; 2 Chron. 19:7,8; Psalm 82). But the question implies they do not. It is not merely acquaintance with the law of the land that is lacking, as if they had not sufficiently studied the law codes they were administering. It is rather practical knowledge. As they claim to be rulers deriving their legitimacy from God's covenant, so their actions and decisions should reflect what is just and proper according to the norms the LORD had established for his people. These norms should have structured the way in which the civil affairs of the land were conducted. Justice, for the prophets, was never merely the product of man's ethical speculation. It was grounded in the revelation of God's will.

We then have a description of their perverse behaviour, for they are those who **hate good and love evil** (*verse 2*). Scripture frequently reminds us of the clear division between good and evil. All too often we, like the people of Micah's day, prefer to fudge issues and consider all grey. But there is no middle ground in the divine evaluation, and we must be forced to come to a decision about the rights and wrongs of our conduct. The rulers were not making abstract statements about hating good and loving evil. It was from their conduct rather than their profession that the judgment was made. 'A tree is recognised by its fruit' (Matt. 12:33).

The picture, then, in the rest of 3:2 and in 3:3 is a brutal one. It goes beyond comparisons made elsewhere of evil rulers to wild animals (Ezek. 22:27; Zeph. 3:3). Some have likened it to cannibalism. Certainly the language is that of butchering an animal whose skin is stripped from it, and the meat separated from the bones. **Who tear the skin from my people and the flesh from their bones** is a picture of callous indifference to human suffering. It is also a picture of exploitation. They **eat my people's flesh, strip off their skin and break their bones in pieces** (*verse 3*). 'Eating people' or 'eating their flesh' was used of the brutal oppression of the wicked (Psalms 14:4; 53:4; Hab. 3:14). Micah builds up the picture in even greater detail so that we may recoil from it with increased revulsion. They **chop them up like meat for the pan, like flesh for the pot**. Perhaps such a description would serve to stir the consciences even of those who were so cruelly exploiting their fellow citizens.

There is here again (see on 1:8,9) a note of the prophet's identification with those who are suffering. They are 'my people' (3:2,3). He identifies with them as they undergo suffering and harsh treatment. The intensity of his language is born out of his sympathy with those who are suffering.

And he envisages a situation of judgment arising. He says **then** (*verse 4*), and **at that time**, but does not specify when that will be. Possibly part of what was originally said has been omitted by Micah, and these other words made the reference clear. Perhaps it refers back to 2:3. We are certainly meant to understand that the day of retribution will not remain an indefinite threat to those whose behaviour does not conform to the norms of the covenant, but will at the time of God's determination surely overtake them.

To cry out to the LORD is used of an appeal to a superior for help in time of trouble. Psalm 107 records the LORD's intervention in response to the cry of his repentant people (Psalm 107:6,13,19,28). **But he will not answer them**. This situation is different (Psalm 18:41; Prov. 28:9; Isa. 1:15; Zech. 7:13). Those who have despised their covenant obligations will not be able to avail themselves of their overlord's assistance in the day of calamity. Their sin separates them from their God (Isa. 59:2,3). **He will hide his face from them** indicates a terrible abandonment by God, when he does not extend his favour to relieve distress (Deut. 31:17,18; Psalm 13:1). **Because of the evil they have done** gives the reason for God's revulsion at their actions and his condemnation of them. It may perhaps go further and express the measure of the divine sentence. It could be translated 'according to all the evil they have done.' His requital is just and fits the crime. They have not listened to those seeking justice when they cried out to them, and so he turns from their entreaties as they suffer.

The second section of the chapter (3:5-8) concerns the prophets – false and true. Micah here records, **This is what the LORD says** (*verse 5*), but it is not clear precisely where the divine speech begins. The NIV starts it immediately **"As for the prophets who lead my people astray"**, and this stresses the LORD's recognition of the bond between himself and his people. An equally valid translation is 'about the prophets who lead my people astray.' In that case we again have Micah speaking out of his fellow feeling for those with whom he personally identifies, and it is the words of judgment from God in 3:6 that are a direct citation.

Now the problem was to recognise a false prophet when you encountered one. These men were not obviously false. They were not Baal prophets, but claimed to speak in the name of the LORD. They were establishment figures, and seem to have been associated with the temple. They were influential, and given a great deal of respect by the rulers of the land. Perhaps these prophets reflect what

happened when the schools of the prophets no longer had an Elijah
or an Elisha at their head. History has certainly shown that no
institutions can degenerate so quickly as theological colleges. The
false prophets were men seeking to perpetuate a theological
tradition. They would quote Scripture, and seek to apply its truth
to their own day. But they quoted only half the message, and their
applications fell short. They failed utterly to see the distinctive
experience that a true prophet like Micah had had.

By describing their self-interested behaviour (Matt. 7:15; Rom.
16:18), the LORD exposes that these men have not been sent by him.
If one feeds them, provides them with money or reward, **then they
proclaim 'peace'**. That is, of course, more than just an absence of
war. 'Peace' embraces a good relationship with God and all the
blessings of the prosperity he bestows. If you paid them enough,
these prophets would say, 'All will be well.' They sanctioned the
conduct of those who paid them, letting them hear what they
wanted to hear. This was not necessarily done in a blatant way. As
3:11 shows, the prophets could and did provide a theological
justification for their words of blessing. But their primary motivation was not to expound the word of God, but material self-interest.
Anyone who did not support them with goods or money became a
target for them. **If he does not, they prepare to wage war against
him**. It is 'sanctify war against him'. In the name of religion and
God, using it to cover their real motives for opposing him, they
would launch a crusade against him.

Therefore (*verse 6*) introduces the divine condemnation that
inevitably ensues. It is a fourfold picture of the blackness and
gloom of disaster (Isa. 8:22). **Night will come over you ... and
darkness ... The sun will set for the prophets, and the day will
go dark for them**. As Amos emphasised, the day of the LORD's
intervention in judgment is 'pitch-dark, without a ray of bright-
ness' (Amos 5:20) for those who are alienated from God. For these
false prophets a further element is added to this extraordinary
darkness in that it will be **without visions**. Night-time was usually
associated with the receiving of visions, but in this situation the

prophets will be unable to provide an explanation for what is going on. It will be **without divination**, which tried to obtain information about the future by examining omens. This was condemned in Israel, though common in surrounding nations. But no matter what method the prophets use to find out about the future, it will not work for them. In the darkness of divine visitation their methods will be shown up for what they are.

So in their failure **the seers will be ashamed and the diviners disgraced** (*verse 7*) leading to shocked despair. **They will all cover their faces** in a gesture of shame or grief (Lev. 13:45; Ezek. 24:17). There is nothing that they can relay to their patrons **because there is no answer from God**. Even their charlatanry fails them.

In the third section of the chapter Micah strongly dissociates himself from such prophets, **But as for me** (*verse 8*). He has not preserved for us any narrative about his call from the LORD, but here he shows us clearly the basis for his being a prophet. Like Paul (compare 2 Cor. 11:10-12; 12:11; Eph. 3:7-9), he does not do this to attract attention to himself, but to vindicate the message he is presenting from the LORD. **I am filled with power, with the Spirit of the LORD, and with justice and might.** The NIV translation fails to show that 'with the Spirit of the LORD' is not expressed in the same way as the other three endowments (compare the translations of the AV and NASB). It is the foundation of his being a prophet of the LORD – his Spirit has come and equipped him for the task. Micah has been given in full measure 'power' to persevere in presenting an unpopular message and opposing what was contrary to the LORD's will (2 Cor. 10:5). 'Justice' (compare 3:1) is that commitment to the standards of the LORD's covenant which was so lacking in Judah's rulers and prophets. That is how Micah knew what was right or wrong, rather than having his perception influenced by bribes (3:11). 'Might' refers to the courage a warrior displays when he goes out unflinchingly to meet the opposing army. The same boldness of speech was displayed by the early church (Acts 4:13,31; Eph. 6:19-20).

These gifts have been given to Micah **to declare to Jacob his**

transgression, to Israel his sin. For the combination of 'Jacob'
and 'Israel' see 2:12, and for 'sin' and 'transgression' see on 1:13.
Micah did not choose his message to win popularity from the rich
and newly influential of his day. His message was given him by
God and was true to the requirements of the covenant. He addressed
the spiritual needs of a community that had twisted aside from
God's standards and forgotten his ways. His task was to confront
them in the LORD's name with their shortcomings.

The mention of Jacob and Israel links in with the following
address to the ruling classes in Jerusalem. **Hear this, you leaders
of the house of Jacob, you rulers of the house of Israel** (*verse 9*).
The description of 3:9 matches that of 3:1-2. In both places there
is a surprising omission. There is no mention of the king, most
likely Hezekiah. Perhaps Micah does not mention him out of
respect for the reforms that he had instituted, though the reforms
did not accomplish all that he wished. But he has no respect for
those in the corridors of power because they **despise justice and
distort all that is right**. 'Despise' is a strong word for expressing
the utter contempt in which they hold God's law and twist to their
own advantage standards of right and wrong (Prov. 17:15).

The administrators **build Zion with bloodshed, and Jerusalem with wickedness** (*verse 10*). This may well refer to the
massive building programmes of Hezekiah's day. There had been
a substantial influx of population from the North after the fall of
Samaria. Archaeological data suggests that in the late eighth
century Jerusalem grew to three or four times its previous size.
Hezekiah also undertook a considerable number of public works in
connection with his moves to defend the city against the Assyrians.
Those who managed these schemes and supervised the forced
labour involved are accused of acting without regard to life
(presumably of the workers) or to the rights of those who owned
land or materials. Later instances of similar behaviour are mentioned in Jeremiah 22:13-16 and Habakkuk 2:12.

**Her leaders judge for a bribe, her priests teach for a price,
and her prophets tell fortunes for money** (*verse 11*) spells out the

venality that controlled the whole of the Jerusalem establishment. The justiciary was corrupt. Decisions went in favour of those who could pay the most. 'A bribe blinds the eyes of the wise and twists the words of the righteous' (Deut. 16:19). The priests had the task of teaching the law of God (Lev. 10:11; Mal. 2:7), but this they will do only if they are paid for it, over and above the ordinary payments made to support them. The prophets' perception of what was required of them was blurred by overwhelming greed. They had become mere fortune tellers.

Yet they lean upon the LORD. The physical act of putting one's weight on a staff or someone's arm for support is used as a metaphor for relying on someone and trusting them for guidance and assistance. The false prophets and the rest of the establishment of Judah did not appreciate how their behaviour had diverged from what the LORD required. 'They claim to know God, but by their actions they deny him' (Titus 1:16). They continued to profess faith in him, and claimed the blessings of the covenant as theirs by right. **Is not the LORD among us? No disaster will come upon us**. They argued that the LORD had given an irrevocable commitment to be with his people and to preserve them. Such a view would have been reinforced by the deliverance of 701 B.C., when Sennacherib had been divinely removed from the gates of Jerusalem (2 Kings 19:35,36). 'The LORD among us' was indeed a precious truth at the heart of Israel's covenant faith (Exod. 17:7; Psalm 46:6; Jer. 14:9), but the requirements of a holy God have to be met for this to be a comfortable truth to be lived with. God had made his blessing on his people dependent on their good conduct (Lev. 26; Deut. 28).

There again follows an announcement of judgment, preceded by **therefore** (*verse 12*) to link their behaviour with the penalty the LORD is imposing. **Because of you** indicates that as a direct result of the perverse reasoning and unjust behaviour displayed by the Jerusalem elite, they were going to experience the opposite of what they claimed would happen. Micah has not up to this point directly spoken of the destruction of the city of Jerusalem. Now, in words that came true with the fall of Jerusalem to the Babylonians in 586

B.C., he says it will be a second Samaria (compare the description in 1:6). The very place they had felt secure will be conquered and devastated. **Zion**, which they had been so corruptly building, **will be ploughed like a field, Jerusalem will become a heap of rubble**. The verbs are passive. No agent is indicated. We are to understand it to be the work of the LORD. How true are the words of Solomon! 'Unless the LORD builds the house, its builders labour in vain' (Psalm 127:1).

The temple hill a mound overgrown with thickets does not just complete the picture of the physical destruction of the city. It indicates the fundamental cause of the disaster. Because of their sin, the LORD has departed from the midst of his people. Consequently the temple which was the symbol of his presence will also be taken away. God has left his people. It is a picture of total spiritual disaster, and one that clashed head on with the theology of the optimistic prophets. One is reminded that after denouncing the teachers of the law and the Pharisees in Matthew 23 for their misuse of their privileges, Jesus foretold the end of the temple that existed in their time (Matt. 24:2). Privilege is the measure of our responsibility, and there is ever the threat of God's chastisement if we do not live up to what we profess.

But there is one bright footnote to this prophecy. So often we wonder if all the prophets said fell on deaf ears. But we know that this prophecy was remembered by the elders of the land a century later and was used to secure Jeremiah's release (Jer. 26:18). This narrative incidentally shows us that in Jeremiah's time Micah was acknowledged as a true prophet of the LORD. Even more significantly, the elders' argument in Jeremiah 26:19 shows the impact of Micah's message in his own day. 'Did not Hezekiah fear the LORD and seek his favour? And did not the LORD relent, so that he did not bring the disaster he pronounced against them?' The LORD gave warning of his impending judgment so that there might be repentance among his people (Jer. 18:7-10). Unfortunately the people did not learn the lesson for long.

Micah 4:1-8: Zion's Exaltation

Our notion of what was involved in being a prophet is very often oriented towards telling what lies in the future. But it is wrong to think of that as the essence of the role of an Old Testament prophet. His task was to be God's covenant messenger, telling the people of the LORD what he wanted them to know. Inevitably, as the LORD is the one who has all history under his control, the messages he gave his spokesmen to deliver could range over the past, the present and the future. But the information about the future was never given merely to satisfy our human craving to know what tomorrow will bring. It was a message controlled and shaped by the LORD's desire either to warn his people against the judgment that would follow if they persisted in their rebellious behaviour, or to encourage those who were loyal to him to remain so despite difficulties and catastrophes. By revealing the glory that yet awaited his people on the other side of the darkness, he strengthened them to endure steadfastly. It is this aspect of the prophetic message that Micah records for us in chapter 4.

There are two parts to the chapter, with a break after 4:8 where the time scale of Micah's vision is altered. In 4:1 he mentions 'the last days', and presumably referring to the same period, he talks in 4:6 of 'that day'. In the original, however, 4:9 begins with the word 'now', and the same word occurs at the start of 4:11, 'but now'. The third stanza of the poem continues in the next chapter and again, in the original, is introduced by 'now' (5:1), but not rendered so in the NIV translation. It would seem that these references to 'now' are about the more immediate future (see on 4:9), whereas in this first section Micah is granted a view further into the future.

In the last days (*verse 1*) points us forward to a time of whose date the prophet is uncertain. The phrase is literally 'at the back of the days', with the future being thought of as behind one, and therefore unable to be perceived. The prophet, however, has been given a view of the future by God. But even on these occasions when God gave such a vision, the precise timing of events was often left obscure (1 Peter 1:10). Indeed the prophet's situation has often been likened to that of an observer looking at a landscape where there is a succession of ever higher hills. From one angle each peak may seem to lie immediately behind the one in front. But move round and look at them from a different viewpoint, and there can often be disclosed hitherto unsuspected valleys – perhaps miles wide – between the successive summits that had at first seemed so close. It may well be that Micah's vision is from the first type of viewpoint. He is not permitted to see the intervening valleys, and so his description merges features of various periods when the LORD will decisively intervene in history. Certainly this prophecy was not exhausted by the return of the Jews from Babylon, though in such an event we can readily detect a partial fulfilment of it.

There is another major interpretative problem that this prophecy poses for us. The prophecy talks about the temple, Zion and Jerusalem. Are we to understand these references as being to sites in Palestine, so that we are being told about some restored Jewish state that will arise before the consummation of all things? There are many problems with such an approach, and it seems preferable to understand Micah as having the future revealed to him in terms of realities that existed in his own day. To make sense to us the future has to be described in terms of what we are already familiar with, even though in retrospect such a description is seen to be deficient in many ways. So for Micah, Israel was the people of God, but that has now been extended and transferred to the church (Gal. 6:16; 1 Peter 2:9,10). The significance of Jerusalem and the temple was that they were where God was pleased to reveal himself in a special way. That role is now taken over by the Christian church (1 Cor. 3:16; Heb. 12:22). The children of Abraham and inheritors of the promises made to the patriarchs are now found throughout the world, wherever the same faith as Abraham's exists (Gal. 3:29). And yet, neither the return of the Jews from Babylon, nor the expansion of the Christian church exhausts this prophecy. They were occasions when the sovereignty and power of the LORD were no longer obscured and acknowledged only by faith, and as such they foreshadowed the ultimate revelation of glory which will be fully realised when the Son of Man returns. It is then that this vision will receive its complete fulfilment.

The picture of the future Micah has revealed to him is painted in terms of features and institutions he already knew well. Incidentally, the prophecy is also found in Isaiah 2:1-4, though we are unable to say definitively with which prophet, if either, it originated. But it may well have been with Micah in that there is an effective contrast between the devastated temple mountain of 3:12 and the glorious mountain (same word in the original) he now describes, **when the mountain of the LORD's temple will be established as chief among the mountains**. The temple was the symbol of the LORD's dwelling with his people, and was where he especially revealed himself to them (1 Kings 8:10,11). It was built on mount Zion, which at 730 metres (2,400 feet) was not particularly high. The passive 'will be established' indicates the action that the LORD takes to ensure that all rivals to him will be seen in their true light. The religions of the ancient world frequently viewed mountains as homes of their gods, and so what is being stressed here is the incomparability of where the LORD has chosen to manifest his presence, and the incomparability of the LORD himself. **It will be raised above the hills** need not refer to a physical exaltation of Zion hill. The truth being conveyed by the imagery is spiritual: the supremacy of the LORD will be incontestably evident (Psalm 68:16).

The picture is not just of future prosperity for Israel. **Peoples will stream to it** envisages a universal recognition of the sovereign rights of the LORD. Israel's religion had always had this universal note. When the LORD called Abraham, he promised him 'all peoples on earth will be blessed through you' (Gen. 12:3), and this wider vision of God's saving purpose was always part of Israel's faith (Psalm 22:27; Isa. 66:20).

Three times a year all Israelite males had to present themselves to worship the LORD at the sanctuary (Deut. 16:16). The pilgrim festivals of Israel will be international in their scope. **Many nations will come and say, "Come, let us go up to the mountain** of the LORD, to the house of the God of Jacob" (*verse 2*). They are presented as doing this with enthusiasm, and also with right motives. (Compare Psalm 122:1.) **He will teach us his ways, so that we may walk in his paths.** It is not as tourists going sightseeing that the nations will come to Jerusalem. They are there as disciples who want to take full advantage of the teaching available in the temple. They are eager to learn how the LORD would have them live their lives in accordance with his will (compare Psalm 25:4).

In the second part of 4:2, Micah adds another dimension to this picture of Zion's exaltation. Not only will all nations converge on Jerusalem, but there will be a reverse movement whereby the standards of the LORD will be disseminated throughout the earth. **The law will go out from Zion, the word of the LORD from Jerusalem.** The word for 'law' is connected with that used for 'teach' in 'he will teach.' It is broader than the commandments of the Mosaic law, and includes all that God has revealed to Israel. That word spreads out in its transforming power as the gospel is proclaimed (Luke 24:47; Acts 1:8; Rom. 15:19).

There are then presented three aspects of what follows on from the international acknowledgment of Zion's God and acceptance of his revealed will.

(1) Nations will no longer have to go to war to settle disputes. This will be done by God. **He will judge between many peoples and will settle disputes for strong nations far and wide** (*verse 3*). A time is envisaged when all reasons for strife will be removed because of a common submission to the standards of the LORD and his enforcement of them (Psalms 96:13; 98:9; Isa. 11:3-5). How magnificent this prospect still seems, but even more so when viewed from Palestine. Over the centuries it has frequently been the battleground for the conflicts of neighbours to the north and south of her.

(2) In a picture that is the opposite of that found in Joel 3:10, national resources will be put to productive rather than military uses. **They will beat their swords into ploughshares and their spears into pruning hooks. Nation will not take up sword**

against nation, nor will they train for war any more. International suspicion and tension result in the stockpiling of weapons, military manoeuvres, and training schools which use up a considerable proportion of a nation's assets. Disarmament releases these resources for better purposes. But we must not forget that the disarmament conference which has brought about these spectacular results has been between the nations and God. They have first to lay aside their hostility toward him, before there can be a true and lasting basis for them laying aside their hostility to one another.

(3) There follows a picture of idyllic satisfaction, again couched in Palestinian terms (Zech. 3:10). **Every man will sit under his own vine and under his own fig tree, and no one will make them afraid** (*verse 4*). Israel had already enjoyed this for a brief period during the reign of Solomon (1 Kings 4:25; 5:4), but it awaited a greater than Solomon to inaugurate it on an international scale. It is not a picture of great riches, but of domestic satisfaction. The ideal is that of contentment with the provision the LORD has made for each, and the opportunity to enjoy it without being harried by others. These arrangements have the best guarantee of all. **The LORD Almighty has spoken.** The LORD Almighty ('the LORD of hosts') is the one who has the powers of the universe under his control and so none will be able to overthrow the arrangements he has instituted.

This evokes the response of Micah's hearers. They profess their loyalty to the LORD despite the situation that surrounds them where **all the nations may walk in the name of their gods** (*verse 5*). This is not to ascribe any legitimacy to their conduct. It is just to recognise that other nations do in fact rely upon and worship other gods. However, the picture of what the LORD will establish strengthens the faith of his people so that they do not fall in with the conduct of the nations that surround them. They deliberately dissociate themselves from them. 'As for us' **we will walk in the name of the LORD our God.** 'Walk' describes the whole conduct of their lives. They will live in faith and obedience, and the phrase 'in the name' probably goes further and brings out the aspect of conscious dependence on the strength of the LORD. It will be **for ever and ever**. Faith sees no end to this loyalty as it perceives no termination to the LORD's provision.

But the picture of future glory has not yet been related to the present condition of the LORD's people. They have indeed voiced their anticipation of it, and now the prophet indicates how they are to get there. **"In that day," declares the LORD** (*verse 6*) links back to 'in the last days' of 4:1, and we are presented with the divine action, as God graciously provides assistance to his stricken people. He does not give them the promise of glory without also assuring them of his action to bring them there.

I will gather the lame resumes the shepherd imagery of 2:12, though the situation has now changed in two respects. It has been located in the more distant future, and the people have experienced the LORD's judgment in full. They are presented as exiles who have been taken from their land in punishment. It is explicitly brought out that they are **those I have brought to grief**. There is no disguising the LORD's chastening hand upon his people because of their sin. But now he acts to gather his afflicted flock. **I will assemble the exiles** is with a view to their restoration (Isa. 35:3-10; Jer. 31:8; Ezek. 34:13). The LORD is dealing with those who have faith and encouraging them even in the experience of divine chastisement of their nation.

I will make the lame a remnant (*verse 7*). The 'lame' do not automatically constitute a remnant, because the word 'remnant' is used here to indicate more than just what has been left. To talk of a remnant after judgment involves hope, because though only part come through unscathed, yet they do in fact come through (2:12). The remnant, though personally weak and incapacitated, are a monument to divine grace. They **had been driven away** by God himself, but they come back **a strong nation. The LORD will rule over them in Mount Zion**. He will be their king in a city and temple restored to their proper status (Psalm 48:1-3). The people of God are told about this to comfort and encourage them to look forward to the eternal rule that will be established **from that day**

and for ever, even as John gives us the description of the new Jerusalem (Rev. 21,22) so that we may eagerly await the return of our Lord (Rom. 8:23).

As for you (*verse 8*) introduces a promise. Who is involved is specified in two titles. **Watchtower of the flock** refers to Jerusalem as the garrison round which the life of the nation revolved as their king looked out and surveyed the affairs of his people. They are 'the flock' of the LORD and Jerusalem will again afford them the security they need. **O stronghold of the Daughter of Zion**. 'Stronghold' or 'hill' (NIV, footnote) refers to Ophel, a fortified mound that had been a feature of Jerusalem since Jebusite days, and which lay to the south of the temple. Mentioning it here again emphasises the protective role Jerusalem played at the centre of Israelite life. The descriptions 'Daughter of Zion' and 'Daughter of Jerusalem' do not refer to a group that is part of, or other than, Zion and Jerusalem. This is rather a Hebrew poetic mode of expression for the population of these places as a whole (Isa. 1:8; Lam. 1:6). The fact that the Hebrew word for 'city' is grammatically a feminine noun made it easy to personify cities as women.

To Jerusalem **the former dominion will be restored; kingship will come to the Daughter of Jerusalem**. The glorious future is seen in terms of the outworking of the promises made to David, 'Your house and your kingdom will endure for ever before me' (2 Sam. 7:16). A king will once more rule in Jerusalem. This is indeed Messianic prophecy in that the expected deliverance is being associated with the figure of a king through whom the LORD will establish his rule over his people.

Blessing will come, but it will only be enjoyed through obedience. Promises given regarding Zion and Jerusalem will not come true merely through human effort. They will come about despite the disobedience of the people and of their king (Psalm 89:30-34), through the restoring grace of God. Those who truly desired the establishment of the LORD's rule are encouraged to look forward to the coming king who would establish the blessing.

Micah 4:9-13: The Road to Restoration

In the previous section Micah had moved on in 4:6 from describing the future glory of Zion to indicating that it would only be by divine intervention that this outcome would be achieved. It is this same theme that is continued in the rest of the chapter, but from a different temporal perspective. There are three stanzas (4:9,10; 4:11-13; 5:1-5), which are linked together by the use of the same initial word 'now' in the Hebrew. Each section focuses on a different aspect of the path from present distress to future glory.

'Now' is not just a formal device to structure the prophetic message. It also alerts us to the fact that the time scale is different from the earlier part of the chapter. There are two ways of understanding the word 'now'.

(1) It could point to the present situation at the time Micah spoke or wrote. In that case the historical occasion of these verses must be different from that of chapter 3, where calamity was prophesied on Jerusalem, but it had not yet arrived. The false prophets were still encouraging the people to believe that no disaster would come upon them. Here that disaster has undoubtedly engulfed the city. Also there is the mention in 4:10 of the command to leave the city, that is, Jerusalem, and that did not happen in Micah's day.

(2) The other, more probable, view is that, as in 3:12, Micah's vision stretches forward over a century to the time of the fall of Jerusalem. He is therefore not using 'now' of the historical circumstances of his own day, but as a way of vividly portraying what was going to happen in the future. Sometimes the prophets do use 'now' in this way, to describe the imminent activity of the LORD (Isa. 33:10; 43:19), or even activity which is still fairly far in the future (Isa. 29:22). Micah himself certainly uses 'now' in this way in 7:10. (See also the comments on 5:4.) He may well have adopted this use of 'now' in this passage to distinguish the time he is talking of from 'the last days' of 4:1 or 'that day' of 4:6. He knows he is viewing a future scene, but one which stands in some way before the ultimate realisation of Zion's glory.

Why do you now cry aloud? (*verse 9*) describes Zion in panic and distress. The descriptions of 4:10,11 indicate that the city has been surrounded and is under siege. The horrors of siege warfare were considerable as famine and plague reduced the inhabitants of the besieged town to walking skeletons unless they capitulated. So it is a cry of alarm and horror that Zion utters. But what note is to be detected in 'Why?': is it suddenness or sarcasm? The answer to that depends largely on how we understand the other question: **Have you no king?** It seems unlikely that the 'king' referred to is the LORD. There are contexts where the LORD is identified as the king who resides in Jerusalem, as when Jeremiah tells of the cry of the people in exile wondering what has happened to them, 'Is not the LORD in Zion? Is her King no longer there?' (Jer. 8:19). But the parallel expression 'your counsellor' is fairly certainly another way of looking at a human king, and to ask, **Has your counsellor perished?** would be an unusual way to refer to the LORD. It seems then that it is the human ruler of Jerusalem that is spoken about.

While the words might refer to the situation that prevailed in the exile, when Israel had no ruling monarch, the question is most probably sarcastic. The city is under siege. The king on whose wisdom and political manoeuvring they had been placing so much hope is unable to think of a way out of their difficulties (Hosea 10:3; 13:10,11). The prophet upbraids them for their previous attitude and questions them sarcastically. 'What has become of your king whose counsel you so much valued? Why are you afraid in your present circumstances, suddenly caught in distress as **pain seizes you like that of a woman in labour**?' It is a crisis to which they are unable to respond because they are overpowered by it. The comparison is one that is frequently found in the Old Testament for a commanding emotional response that leaves one unable to cope with a situation (Isa. 13:8; 21:3; 26:17; Jer. 22:23; 50:43). They are unable to alleviate or deflect their agony.

Then Micah tells Zion that that is how she should indeed act. **Writhe in agony, O Daughter of Zion, like a woman in labour** (*verse 10*). For 'Daughter of Zion', see on 4:8. The situation they will encounter will truly justify such a response, for they will be experiencing the LORD's judgment. **Now, in the future situation envisaged, you must leave the city to camp in the open field**. They had been relying on the false prophets' views of the future. They taught the people that Zion was inviolate, and that they should look back to how the LORD had delivered his people in the past. But Micah reminds them that an Exodus-style deliverance has to be from a foreign land.

You will go to Babylon. Babylon was a significant city in the Assyrian empire, but it was not its capital. This has led many to suspect that this passage is not from Micah's day when Assyria was the aggressor and the future resurgence of Babylon was as yet unanticipated. In view of the way this statement is integrated into its context, it is quite improbable that it was inserted at some later time. Rather we should question the assumptions made about the prevailing perception of Babylon. Babylonian envoys had already come to Hezekiah (Isa. 39), and it is very likely that mention of Babylon in this context of exile shows Micah's familiarity with the prophecy Isaiah had delivered to Hezekiah probably around 705 B.C. 'The time will surely come when everything in your palace, and all that your fathers have stored up until this day, will be carried off to Babylon' (Isa. 39:6). Although he will later return to consider Assyria again, the vision granted Micah at this point enables him to relate the circumstances that will prevail at the time of the exile (586 B.C.). It would be some time before events would demonstrate the falsity of the majority teaching of his own day.

There is twice emphasised in 4:10 to show that it would not be Jerusalem, as was falsely supposed, that would be the scene of the LORD's intervention to deliver his people in the new Exodus. **You will be rescued. The LORD will redeem you out of the hand of your enemies**. 'Rescue' (Exod. 5:23; 18:9,10) and 'redeem' (Exod. 6:6; 15:13) would have taken the minds of the people of Judah back to the events of the Exodus, which formed the basic model for them to grasp what it meant to have God act as their Saviour. He intervenes to rescue his people when they are helpless. Redemption speaks of God's restoring what was once his to its rightful position. The enemies' power will not be a match for the

LORD's. Although he will have used their enemies to chastise his people, judgment will not be his last word. They will be restored, but in such a way as to ensure that all the glory accords to the LORD.

The second stanza of the poem (4:11-13) presents the same cycle of the LORD's people facing disaster and his subsequent intervention to overthrow the plans of those who plot against them. The situation resembles that described in Psalm 2, where the peoples plot in vain against the king of Israel and his God. They do not know that the Lord enthroned in heaven is looking with disdainful laughter at their puny efforts to overthrow the ruler he has established. Judah is being taught to look on her situation from the perspective of heaven.

But now (*verse 11*) brings us back again to the city under siege. It is no minor disaster that would engulf Judah because of the LORD's judgment against her. **Many nations are gathered against you.** The armies of the empires of the day included troops drawn from many different subject peoples. No doubt their various modes of dress marked out the composite nature of those who gathered against Jerusalem. This would serve to emphasise her isolation and seeming helplessness in political terms (Jer. 1:15).

The prophet quotes what would be on the lips of the invading troops. **They say, "Let her be defiled, let our eyes gloat over Zion!"** Their plan is not just to capture and loot her, but to defile her. Presumably this refers to the way they would treat the temple and its precincts. They come haughtily against the LORD's dwelling place, because they act as those who are in defiant rebellion against him. They yearn with malicious desire to gloat over Zion when they have humiliated her. What she experiences arises out of her relationship with the LORD, for the animosity of the enemy is not primarily directed against her but her God (John 15:20).

However, there is another dimension to the situation, one of which the enemy forces are ignorant. **But they do not know the thoughts of the LORD; they do not understand his plan** (*verse 12*). The LORD is using them. He has permitted them to gather against his people, but it is what he wills, and that alone, which will come to pass. In their proud self-confidence they are blind to what is really happening. In fact the LORD is the one **who gathers them like sheaves to the threshing floor**. Threshing floors were open areas of hard ground usually outside the city wall, where the sheaves were taken to be chopped up and the grain loosened by the threshing sledge. An army encamped in siege against a city would often occupy the site used for threshing in more peaceful times.

Then the LORD addresses his people, **O Daughter of Zion**, in the first part of 4:13. He commands them to **rise and thresh**. The threshing would usually be done by an ox pulling the sledge behind it. But the picture seems to change from this. **I will give you horns of iron** conveys the power with which the LORD will endow his people for the task for which he commissions them. **I will give you hoofs of bronze and you will break to pieces many nations**. One is reminded of the victory assured to the Messiah (Psalm 2:8,9) because of what the LORD has given him.

The closing words of the verse seem to be those of the prophet himself as he describes the victory that will be granted to the LORD's people. **You will devote their ill-gotten gains to the LORD, their wealth to the Lord of all the earth**. He has seen the promised victory, and is sure of it. He talks rather of the allocation of the spoil. It will be done under the rules of sacred warfare. The enemy's loot will be presented to the LORD and for his service (Isa. 18:7; 60:6-10). It is his by right, for he is 'the Lord of all the earth.' 'Lord' here is Adon, 'master' (as in 1:2), not Yahweh, the covenant name for God. Its use may be a deliberate rejection of the unwarranted claims of some of the pagan rulers. Sennacherib certainly used for himself the title 'King of the world'. But he who truly is 'the King of kings and Lord of lords' (1 Tim. 6:15) is here presented with the booty his conquering people have captured.

Micah 5:1-6: The Ruler from Bethlehem

Although the NIV translation does not reproduce the word 'now', Micah uses it to begin 5:1 as he had in 4:9 and 4:11 earlier. For the third time he traces out the path by which Zion's fortunes will be transformed from the hopelessness of siege and exile by the wonder of the LORD's deliverance. But he does not simply repeat the message: each time he looks at matters from a different perspective. The first time he had shown how an Exodus style deliverance would require the people to be in a foreign land, exiled in Babylon. The second time he emphasised the LORD's control over what was happening even though those involved would not be aware of it. Now in the third, culminating description he is able to give a clear picture of the one through whom the LORD will restore the fortunes of his people. Perhaps this is the best known part of Micah's prophecy, when he tells of the Messiah, the kingly ruler, who would come from Bethlehem.

But before he introduces the Messiah, Micah again addresses Zion under siege. **Marshal your troops, O city of troops** (*verse 1*) may also be rendered as 'Strengthen your walls, O walled city' (as in the NIV footnote). The latter follows the Septuagint, the ancient Greek translation of the Old Testament, and involves a slight change in the Hebrew text. The city is clearly Zion. Literally, the address is 'daughter of troops', and is a development of the phrase 'daughter of Zion' (4:10; 4:13) in the previous two pictures, using a Hebrew idiom that means 'warlike city'. Micah has used the terminology of war to describe the crimes perpetrated in Jerusalem (2:8), and perhaps this usage here is ironically contrasting their willingness to engage in warlike activity against their own countrymen with the need to organise themselves to meet the enemy's assault on their city because **a siege is laid against us**. The prophet again identifies with the people, as he does also at the end of the section in 5:6 'our land' and 'our borders'. What happens to them is something that necessarily affects him also.

When did this occur? Some have suggested the reference is to the siege of Jerusalem in 701 B.C. by Sennacherib. More probably this is a continuation of the series looking forward to the downfall of Jerusalem more than a century later. **They will strike Israel's**

ruler on the cheek with a rod points to the utter personal
humiliation of the individual who is incapable of defending his face
(Job 16:10; Psalm 3:7; Lam. 3:30). It seems to take place after the
capture of the city, which did not happen in Hezekiah's day. The
word 'ruler' is the same as that used for the judges of Israel after
Joshua's time. But this ruler of God's people Israel (the reference
is to Judah as the people of God) is unlike the judges of old – he
cannot deliver the people. He is unable to rescue himself from
personal abuse. The rod which should have functioned as the
symbol of his royal authority (Psalm 2:9; Isa. 14:5) is, as it were,
snatched from him and used to beat him.

Micah, however, turns from the depressing spectacle of Israel's
humiliated king by citing a saying of the LORD which presents a
startling contrast. **But you, Bethlehem Ephrathah** (*verse 2*) points
away from the besieged city to a place whose very names Bethlehem,
'house of bread', and Ephrathah, 'fertile area', conjure up a vision of
prosperity. Ephrathah was an older name for Bethlehem (Gen. 35:19;
48:7) and was also used for the surrounding area. **You are small
among the clans of Judah**. The focus is not so much on its physical
size, as on its political insignificance. In terms of the traditional
subdivisions of the tribe of Judah it had not been very important.

But though as a place Bethlehem had not been particularly well
known, it was the birthplace of David, who had been the king after
God's own heart (1 Kings 9:4; 11:6). So in looking for a new ruler,
the LORD says he will go back to the same outwardly unpromising
beginning and **out of you will come ... one who will be ruler over
Israel.** This is the Messiah, in whom the promises of the Davidic
covenant are realised (2 Sam. 7:12-16), a king who will be the
means of restoring and exercising the LORD's rule over his people.
But the word 'king' is not used here, probably to emphasise the
Messiah's acceptance of his subordinate role and his willingness to
rule on behalf of the LORD and in his interests. **For me** is given
special emphasis, and it, along with the notion of going back to
Bethlehem, involves an implicit rejection of later kings who had
made their own interests paramount.

Following upon this, we have the enigmatic words **whose origins are from of old, from ancient times**. The NIV translation conveys the truly royal ancestry of the Messiah. The LORD is not rejecting the house of David, but will establish as king one who is a legitimate descendant of that venerable line. But it is possible that the words indicate more than that. The phrase translated 'from ancient times' may be rendered 'from days of eternity', as in the NIV footnote, and could be understood as an ascription of eternal origins to this Ruler. However, 'whose origins' is literally 'his goings forth', picking up the similar word 'he shall go forth' earlier in the verse. It is more probable then that rather than directly indicating something of the personal, eternal origins of this Ruler, the word shows that his acts of going forth do not start with his future appearance, but have already been of old, even from days of eternity or of antiquity. It is in the latter sense that Micah uses the same phrase in 7:14. On either rendering, he expects a more than human figure. He will come in the future, yet his goings forth have also been in the remote past.

Therefore (*verse 3*) serves to bring out the implications of the way the LORD is going to deliver. The Messiah is going to come forth out of lowly circumstances at a time when the Davidic line will have receded into obscurity. In the meantime, however, **Israel will be abandoned** by God to devastation by her enemies and to exile, when her rightful kings will not reign over her. But it will be a limited abandonment. Two conditions are stated to establish its duration.

(1) It will be **until the time when she who is in labour gives birth**. In the light of the prophecy in Isaiah 7:14, which would have preceded Micah's by about thirty years, this may be a reference to Mary. But taken in the context of this threefold cycle of predictions, 'she who is in labour' may just as readily point back to a 'woman in labour' (4:9,10) which refers to Zion undergoing pain and agony until from within her there is born the Messiah (Rev. 12:2).

(2) The second condition is that the people will be abandoned until **the rest of his brothers return to join the Israelites**. Despite the hostility that had often existed between the Northern and

Southern Kingdoms, Judah felt it deeply when her brothers in the North were deported. This condition reflects their desire for the people to be reunited. It is as they are brought together again into one that Israel's abandonment by God is brought to an end, and the LORD shows how completely he can reverse the effects of human sin. This was partially fulfilled in the return from the Exile, but supremely so in Christ in whom the whole building is joined together (Eph. 2:21). The Messiah's kingdom is not completely established until there is the unity and harmony of one fold and one Shepherd (Ezek. 37:22; John 10:16).

This thought is taken further in the following description of the Messiah. **He will stand** (*verse 4*) is probably a picture of regal majesty. He **will shepherd his flock**. While the kings of the east frequently took the title of Shepherd, its use in the Old Testament recalls the way in which David was taken by God from being a literal shepherd to oversee his people (2 Sam. 5:2; 7:7,8; Psalm 78:70-72). The king who will come will shepherd the people with tenderness and consideration (Isa. 40:11; 49:10; Matt. 12:15-21). His success will stem from his recognition that the essential feature of a true king over the LORD's covenant people is that he does not act in his own strength, but **in the strength of the LORD**. He will draw from divine resources to provide for his people. **In the majesty of the name of the LORD his God** shows that his reign will be clothed in splendour because of the authority given him by the LORD (Psalms 93:1; 145:12) with whom he lives in especially close relationship so that he may be in a particular way called 'his God'.

Their king's true awareness of and responsiveness to the demands of the covenant bring blessing for his people. **They will live securely**, enjoying the benefits that having him for their king involves. **For then** (literally it is 'now', but obviously it refers to the future time of which the prophet is speaking) **his greatness will reach to the ends of the earth**. The dominion of the Messiah will be the actuality what had always been dreamed of for the monarchs of Israel – a universal empire (Psalms 2:8; 22:27; 72:8; Zech. 9:10).

The way in which the text of 5:5 is printed in the NIV shows that it is easier to decide where this section of Micah's prophecy begins than where it ends. Many make a break in the middle of the verse so that the words **And he will be their peace** (*verse 5*) conclude the section by emphasising all that the Messiah will be to his people. 'Peace' here involves more than just cessation of warfare (Psalm 72:7; Isa. 9:6). It covers that total well-being before God which Paul has in mind when he says of Christ, 'He is our peace' (Eph. 2:14).

There are, however, good reasons to respect the way in which the Hebrew text treats the passage, with no break in 5:5. The two verses 5:5,6 then give a practical illustration of the way in which the Messiah destroys his people's enemies to ensure they can live securely. The introductory words 'He will be their peace' match the words towards the end of 5:6 'he will deliver us' and serve to bracket the verses together. Indeed the prophet's use of 'us' and 'our' at the end of 5:6 serves a similar function in bringing out the unity of this section, as this act of identification with the people and their interests picks up that which he had displayed in 5:1.

But there are problems in interpreting the passage. The references to Assyria seem to imply that Micah is talking again about the invasion that took place in 701 B.C. It is just about possible to read 5:5b-6a as the vain boasting of the people that when the Assyrian comes, as they expected he shortly would, there would be a sufficiency of men capable of defeating him. 'Shepherds' and 'leaders of men' refer to those with the ability to rule and guide the forces of Judah. 'Seven... even eight' is an idiom that suggests multiplicity (Eccles. 11:2), as does 'six... even seven' (Job 5:19; Prov. 6:16). The people seem to say, 'We have an abundance of military skill and prowess. We will be so successful we will crush and rule the land of Assyria with the sword.' Against this boastful self-confidence, the prophet would then say, 'He will deliver us', directing the people to the God-given ruler who alone can deliver when the enemy threatens the people of God.

But a superior way of understanding these verses is to take Assyria, the enemy of God's people which Micah's contemporaries knew all about, as representative of all the enemies of God's people. Micah uses 'Assyria' in this typical fashion in 7:12 also, where the people when they are restored to the land are said to come from Assyria, the land of their enemies, even though that empire would have completely disappeared by then. (This is a theme that is taken up in great detail by Nahum, for example in Nahum 1:14.) Zechariah also uses 'Assyria' (and 'Egypt') in Zechariah 10:10 to represent the nations from whom the LORD will gather his people when he restores them. Such a typical usage is made more probable in this passage by the mention of 'the land of Nimrod' in 5:6, who is otherwise mentioned only in Genesis 10:8-12 and 1 Chronicles 1:10. The Genesis passage refers to Babylon as well as Nineveh (Assyria).

On this approach, the prophet represents himself as joining with those who have sworn allegiance to the Messiah as the one who secures the peace of his people. **When the Assyrian invades our land and marches through our fortresses** which he has taken, they confess that in this situation of their enemies' advance against them, they will be provided by their king with a wealth of talented leadership who will ensure their victory over their enemies. **We will raise against him seven shepherds, even eight leaders of men**, not as a display of merely human resources, but by divine gift. The people of God are still under attack, and have to be ready to fight, even though they 'do not wage war as the world does' (2 Cor. 10:3). Their enemies are 'the powers of this dark world' and 'the spiritual forces of evil in the heavenly realms' (Eph. 6:12). Nor are they left to fight relying on their own resources. The risen Christ who is the peace of his people gives his church those who will pastor and teach it so that it is ready for action (Eph. 4:11,12).

The action that is fought is not solely defensive. **They will rule the land of Assyria with the sword, the land of Nimrod with drawn sword** (*verse 6*). In their victory the leaders of the people crush the land of their enemies. Similarly today the spiritual battle involves more than resisting the inroads of the enemy. Paul tells the Corinthians, 'The weapons we fight with are not the weapons of the world. On the contrary, they have divine power to demolish strongholds. We demolish arguments and every pretension that sets itself up against the knowledge of God, and we take captive every thought to make it obedient to Christ' (2 Cor. 10:4,5).

The source of success is still the same. Those who act as under-shepherds to the Messianic King are not credited with the success of their endeavours. Rather, **he will deliver us from the Assyrian when he invades our land and marches into our borders**. The strength to obtain the victory comes from him. 'I can do everything through him who gives me strength' (Phil. 4:13).

Micah 5:7-15: The Victory of the Remnant

Micah brings the second main division of his prophecy to a conclusion by exploring further the role the people of God have to play in the victory that the Ruler from Bethlehem will gain. This has already been touched on in 5:5,6, but now it is spelled out in greater detail. First there are two contrasting pictures of the function assigned to the remnant of Jacob in connection with other nations. They both benefit many people ('the dew', 5:7), and overwhelm them ('the lion', 5:8,9). Then from 5:10 to the end of the chapter the spotlight falls on the condition of the LORD's people themselves. It is emphasised that it is only by way of purity and obedience that they will be able to participate in the LORD's universal victory (Eph. 5:3-5; Rev. 22:14,15). He works holiness in them, removing all that pollutes, so that they are fit for his service.

Micah uses two deftly drawn illustrations to describe the part which **the remnant of Jacob** (*verse 7*) will play. 'Remnant', as has been seen (2:12; 4:7), points beyond the calamities that would overtake the people in the LORD's judgment. It indicates that only some, not all, will come through the experience of the LORD's chastening hand upon the nation. Still some do come through, and the future verb **will be** points beyond the disaster to the restoration inaugurated by the Messiah. Then the remnant will function strategically in the furtherance of his kingdom.

On its own the phrase **in the midst of many peoples** might suggest that the remnant is once again found as a nation surrounded by others, but it is perhaps more in keeping with the comparisons that follow to view it as spread through the nations. It is going to influence the world **like dew from the LORD, like showers on the grass**. A similar description is also found of the benefits of the rule of the Messianic king (Psalm 72:6). In the dry climate of Palestine dew played a significant role in providing moisture for the growing crops, and could frequently be very heavy. The 'showers' were not light rain, but heavy, probably what came in the spring and permitted growth to start. Both the dew and the showers **do not wait for man or linger for mankind**. They are not under human control, but are part of God's provision for the natural good of the land. So the remnant that he preserves is going to be accorded a divine role in the destiny of the nations. Spread among them, it will exercise a spiritual ministry patterned after that of the Messiah. It will disseminate knowledge about God and call on the nations to turn to him. In this way it will fulfil what had been promised to Abraham: 'Through your offspring all nations on earth will be blessed' (Gen. 22:18).

The beginning of 5:8 is structured in a very similar way to the beginning of 5:7. **The remnant of Jacob will be among the nations, in the midst of many peoples** (*verse 8*). No longer, however, is the picture one of the beneficent influence of the people of God. The focus is now on a contrasting ministry. It will be **like a lion among the beasts of the forest, like a young lion among flocks of sheep, which mauls and mangles as it goes, and no one can rescue**. The lion was a figure that had been used of God's people in the past (Num. 23:24; 24:9), as those whose power would vanquish their foes. The remnant, even though its numbers are diminished, executes that role because it will be divinely empowered. When the LORD is with his people, there is no force that is able to resist and to oppose them effectively (Rom. 8:31-39).

But when does this take place? What is the realisation of this prophecy? Its position in this chapter places it after the appearance of the Messiah, and it is therefore a consequence of his rule. It may best be understood as the part that the church – both of Jewish and Gentile extraction – plays as the true children of Abraham (Gal. 3:29), taking on the mantle of God's people and bringing their role forward to its fulfilment. As the people of God are spread among the many nations of the earth (Acts 1:8; 1 Peter 1:1), they are an irresistible force that affects for good or ill, all with whom they come in contact. As Paul writes, 'We are to God the aroma of Christ among those who are being saved and those who are perishing. To the one we are the smell of death; to the other, the fragrance of life' (2 Cor. 2:15,16).

The church's divinely assigned activity has triumphant consequences. **Your hand will be lifted up in triumph over your enemies, and all your foes will be destroyed** (*verse 9*). These words may also be translated as an exhortation, 'Lift up your hands in triumph over your enemies'. In the light of the task given her, the church is not to be passive but to go on and enter whole-heartedly into the role that the LORD has assigned her, because her victory is certain. The note is that of confidence in the victory the LORD will provide as in 4:13.

But there is a major condition that must be fulfilled before the people will be able to enter into the triumph presented here. There must be holiness prevalent among them (Zeph. 3:13). They must be the people of God in more than name. Their attitudes and behaviour will have to be such as to warrant that exalted title, and from 5:10 onwards God states that he will act to ensure that this condition is met.

In that day (*verse 10*) does not seem to link directly back to the immediately preceding verses, as if only after the victory is won, will God act to ensure his people's holiness. Micah does not introduce this divine saying here because it is the temporal consequence of what has immediately preceded. It links back to 'that day' of 4:6,7, to the time when the LORD prepares the remnant so that they may be suitable and effective servants. By positioning the saying at this point in his prophecy, Micah is providing an effective application of the message of the coming Messianic reign to the situation of his own day. He has shown the glorious prospect that is in store for those who are loyal to the LORD, and now he points out to his hearers that the loyalty required is that of obedience. He is in effect saying to them that if you want to participate in the blessings God will provide, you must now reform your behaviour so that it coincides with what he expects of those who are in covenant with him. This is still the standard of behaviour that God demands (Gal. 5:19-21).

I will destroy uses the same verb that is translated 'cut off' in passages such as Leviticus 17:10; 20:3,5. It indicates the action that the LORD takes to remove from his people those who are themselves impure and so pollute the community of the LORD. In this way the LORD preserves for himself a people who can truly honour him. The thinking that lies behind this is expressed clearly in Leviticus 20:6-8: 'I will set my face against the person who turns to mediums and spiritists to prostitute himself by following them, and I will cut him off from his people. Consecrate yourselves and be holy, because I am the LORD your God. Keep my decrees and follow them. I am the LORD, who makes you holy.' This is the sanctifying work of God to render his people fit for his service. The fourfold repetition of 'I will destroy' along with the other words for removal bring out the extent to which the land has been polluted and the thoroughness with which the LORD purges his people.

He first says that he will destroy **your horses from among you and demolish your chariots**. This is not intended to leave his people defenceless, but to remove from them a source of false confidence, as was indicated in discussing 1:13. Scripture does not prohibit the use of legitimate means, but it has no place for putting confidence in false means. Cavalry and light war-chariots were the ultimate in military hardware in those days. God wishes his people to find their security in him and not in the equipment they provide for themselves. They must make David's sentiment their own: 'Some trust in chariots and some in horses, but we trust in the name of the LORD our God' (Psalm 20:7). In that way they will know how to stand firm in the day of testing (Psalm 33:16-22).

I will destroy the cities of your land and tear down all your strongholds (*verse 11*). This too looks at the military preparations in which they were placing their trust. A city was, of course, a fortified place, and the inhabitants were liable to find themselves looking to the strength of their walls for security rather than to the LORD. 'Strongholds' also refers to the cities of the land, as places that were designed to hold out against enemy invasion. Quite apart from their fortifications, they were often built on steeply sloping hills.

In 5:12 the LORD states that he will act to remove anything pertaining to the occult from his people. **I will destroy your witchcraft and you will no longer cast spells** (*verse 12*). The evidence of Isaiah 2:6 shows the extent to which Judah was permeated by these foreign influences in Micah's day. They represent attempts by man to gain knowledge of the future in ways which were forbidden to Israel, and must be removed to ensure that the people are blameless before God (Deut. 18:9-13). The people had to resist those who inveigle them into such pagan practices. God's law and testimony should be their only guide (Isa. 8:19,20).

I will destroy your carved images and your sacred stones from among you (*verse 13*). God now focuses on the idolatry that was prevalent in the land. This had been the root cause of Samaria's downfall (1:7) and he is not going to permit any trace of it to remain among his restored people. 'Carved images' were sculptured out of wood, stone, or metal. Images of the LORD fell under the condemnation of the Second Commandment (Exod. 20:4) lest the people fall into the error of thinking that they could manipulate God through the image they had made. But here it is more probable that the images purported to be of other deities and this was prohibited by the requirements of the First Commandment (Exod. 20:3). 'Sacred stones' were erected in Canaanite sanctuaries as symbols of the male deity that was being worshipped. **You will no longer bow down to the work of your hands**. The prophets frequently presented scathing attacks on the absurdity of people worshipping idols they had produced for themselves (Isa. 44:9-21; Jer. 10:3-10).

The first part of 5:14 continues with the removal of other aspects of the customary equipment of Canaanite shrines. **I will uproot from among you your Asherah poles** (*verse 14*). These wooden poles, sometimes the trunks of trees, were symbols of Asherah, a goddess who was widely worshipped in the East. As they were fixed in the ground, the idea of their being 'uprooted' is an appropriate symbol of their desecration. The continuation of 5:14 **and demolish your cities** has presented a challenge to scholars, with no very satisfactory solution being brought forward. The problem is that the phrase in the second half of the verse does not seem to balance that in the first part, as occurs in the other verses of this highly polished sequence. No one knows what has happened. The text as it stands really reverts to the idea of 5:11.

Then there is a final statement by the LORD. **I will take vengeance in anger and wrath upon the nations that have not obeyed me** (*verse 15*). Whereas in the previous verses we have the action of the LORD to cleanse his people from all that was polluting them, we now find the focus turns to his actions against the other nations who have refused to obey him (Psalm 149:7). 'Vengeance' can easily mislead us because we often think of it in terms of blood-feuds and vendettas that cause untold misery. But this is the LORD asserting his rights as sovereign ruler. It is the consequence of the title accorded him in 4:13 'the Lord of all the earth'. But the nations have not recognised his lordship by obeying his commands. The time will then come when he will vindicate his rule and his claims upon their obedience, by punishing their continued rebellion. They have mistaken the situation if they think that he has been viewing their rebellion with indifference. He has been treating them with long-suffering. But now they will experience his 'anger and wrath' at the way they have despised and set aside his claims on them (2 Thess. 2:8-10). When the LORD has prepared his people so that they are ready to serve him in holiness, he will also act to secure the punishment of those who have rejected his claims upon them and despised his authority.

Micah 6:1-8: The LORD's Indictment

As Micah begins the third part of his book, he turns back from unfolding the deliverance the LORD would provide for his people, to pressing home the reality of their present rebellion and estrangement from him. As before (compare 1:2; 3:1), Micah starts this major part of his book with a summons, **Listen to what the LORD says** (*verse 1*). What then follows takes the form of a legal indictment based on the covenant relationship the LORD had instituted between himself and his people at Sinai (Deut. 5:2).

Covenant is one of the major theological metaphors of Scripture. The LORD used it to teach Israel to think of the relationship between himself and them in terms of the relationships that existed in contemporary international treaties between emperors (suzerains) and their subject peoples (vassals). The emperors of the ancient world were no different from their later counterparts in viewing with disfavour any behaviour that indicated a lessening of their subjects' loyalty to their regime. Their treaties therefore strictly forbade behaviour that could be construed as rebellious, or over-friendly to other powers. Consequently, 'treaty' or 'covenant' became a pervasive religious metaphor in Israel alone among the peoples of the Ancient Near East, because polytheistic beliefs did not give scope for an exclusive loyalty such as characterised Israel in their unique engagement to serve only Yahweh, their covenant LORD.

The use of analogies drawn from the sphere of international relations is taken further in the ministry of the prophets. Just as a suzerain would send a messenger to convey his orders to his vassals, so too the covenant LORD sent his messengers the prophets (2 Chron. 36:15,16; Hag. 1:13) to remind his people of the provision he had already made for them, and what he still intended to do for, and through, them. The prophets also, as God's diplomatic messengers, spelled out the obedience Israel should render in gratitude to their covenant king.

When a country failed to please its overlord, it was often the case that, rather than despatching troops to straighten things out, the emperor would first of all send a messenger. His task was to charge the people with their misdemeanours and see if threats of punishment would recall them to loyalty and obedience. It is this pattern of behaviour, often termed a 'covenant lawsuit' (compare Isa. 1:18; Jer. 2:9; Hosea 4:1), that is being used here to teach Judah how the LORD is dealing with them. Yahweh, as Israel's king, is pressing charges against his people for their infringement of the terms of the covenant between them. If they accept the situation and repent, then they may be restored to the king's favour. The object of the covenant lawsuit is to recall them to loyalty, as can be seen in 6:8 which ends the section on a note of pleading, rather than by threatening judgment.

One Scriptural example of a secular diplomat engaged on a similar mission is to be found in the speech of the Rabshakeh ('field commander', NIV) as part of the campaign of the Assyrians against Hezekiah in 701 B.C. (2 Kings 18:17-25; Isa. 36:1-10). Indeed, it is possible that Micah first presented this message around that time, saying in effect, 'You have heard the warnings of Sennacherib's messenger. Now hear the far more serious warnings of Yahweh's messenger.' The circumstances in Jerusalem would have given the message an added force.

After the initial summons to get his hearers' attention, Micah continues by relating the commission the Lord had given him. (The quotation marks in the NIV should be closed at the end of 6:1.) **Stand up, plead your case**. These commands are singular and addressed to Micah, as can be seen in the AV translation, 'Arise, contend thou.' Micah has been delegated to act as the LORD's spokesman in legal proceedings. But what that case is, is not immediately revealed. Micah keeps his hearers in suspense by withholding the name or names of the persons involved.

The witnesses, however, are solemnly named, and this shows that what is in dispute is no light or trivial matter. Micah is told to initiate proceedings **before the mountains; let the hills hear what you have to say**. Mention of the mountains and the hills reflects another feature of ancient covenant making procedure. Witnesses were invoked at the making of the covenant, and in pagan cultures these were normally gods and goddesses. In Israel that was not an option, so heaven and earth are frequently called upon to play the same role (Deut. 4:26; 32:1; Isa. 1:2). If they could speak, they would testify to the undertakings given by both parties.

It is Micah who then speaks. He fulfils his commission as the LORD's prosecutor, and enjoins the witnesses to pay attention. **Hear, O mountains, the LORD's accusation; listen, you everlasting foundations of the earth** (*verse 2*). 'The everlasting foundations' (or, 'enduring foundations') refers to the mountains, looked upon as supporting the earth, with roots going deep into the soil (see Jonah 2:6). They have been in existence for a long time, and thus may bear testimony both to what the LORD had required in his covenant and how the people had in fact responded.

It is only in the second part of 6:2 that the parties to the dispute are clearly announced. It is the LORD versus his people. **The LORD has a case against his people**. He is putting into formal procedure his complaint against them – the ones who should be loyal to him, because he had saved them and claimed them as his own. **He is lodging a charge against Israel**. Israel is the covenant name of the people, even though it is only those in the Southern Kingdom who by this time are left to be cited to appear. It is not, however, a matter of an open-and-shut case. There is still the possibility of a rejoinder from the defence. The verb translated as 'to lodge a charge' is closely related to that translated 'let us reason together' in a similar context in Isaiah 1:18.

The Divine Accusation (6:3-5). Micah here directly quotes the LORD speaking to his people. In 6:3 and 6:5 the LORD calls them **My people**, and emphasises the bond that existed between them. Covenant was not just a formal legal procedure. It was intended to establish a friendly, loving relationship between the parties. It was not to be thought of on the lines of a contract between business partners, but more as a marriage bond between parties pledging themselves to each other. This form of address in itself constitutes a reminder and a rebuke.

The LORD's indictment is remarkable in what it does not do. It does not present a catalogue of Israel's misdemeanours. Rather than listing their transgressions, it focuses on what the LORD had done for them. The behaviour of the people should have reflected their relationship to him, and when their behaviour is wrong, it shows up a faulty understanding of where they were in relation to him. They did not appreciate all that he had done for them as a nation.

What have I done to you? (*verse 3*) asks if there was any charge they could levy against him that would justify their attitude towards him? A clue as to what Israel's attitude had been is found in the question, **How have I burdened you?** Israel felt their relationship with the LORD wearisome. They were tired out by the demands and restrictions they felt that he had placed on their living. They had no spiritual freshness or joy. They found the LORD, and by implication also the word that his prophet brought, unnecessarily tiresome and tedious.

But this was a travesty of reality. **Answer me**, or 'Testify against me', clearly implies that though this was the way they were thinking and speaking, it could not be backed up by evidence. It is a legal challenge to be specific and prove what they are alleging. It puts the people on the defensive.

God then reminds them of what he had done. **I brought you up out of Egypt** (*verse 4*). In Hebrew the words 'I burdened you' (6:3) and 'I brought you up' (6:4) are very similar in sound, and serve to bring out the contrast between the allegations made and the facts of the case. 'Far from pressing you down, I released you.' This looks back to the events of the Exodus, where the LORD had demonstrated his care for Israel. His action constituted his claim upon them, as the introduction to the Ten Commandments in Exodus 20:1 reminded them, '**I redeemed you from the land of slavery**'. The Exodus is the basic Old Testament model for the salvation the LORD provides (4:10). God says, 'That is what I provided for you — freedom by paying the redemption price that was needed to achieve it.' We also see here, as in many other places in the Old Testament (for instance, Deut. 5:2,3; 29:14,15), the people of God viewed as a single entity over the centuries. Micah's contemporaries were the current representatives of the one covenant people of God. What had happened in the past was not to be written off as ancient history, but rather prized as the basis of their present privileges.

What the LORD had provided for his people had not been mere escape. **I sent Moses to lead you, also Aaron and Miriam**. No one doubted the standing of these great leaders of Israel in the past. They exemplified the quality of the LORD's provision for his people – and perhaps mentioning them was intended to stir up questions about why they were not still blessed with similarly outstanding leaders.

The LORD repeats his affectionate address, **My people** (*verse 5*). They are urged to **remember what Balak king of Moab counselled and what Balaam son of Beor answered**. The incidents referred to are recorded in Numbers 22-24, and remind them of the LORD's further provision when they were almost baulked at the entrance to the land. He protected them from their adversaries, and frustrated the schemes of their enemies to have them cursed so that they would be defeated.

Remember your journey from Shittim to Gilgal. This refers to the crossing of the Jordan when the Israelites came into the promised land. Shittim was the last place on the east bank of the Jordan where the people camped for a long time (Num. 33:49; Josh. 3:1), and Gilgal was the first encampment they had on the west bank (Josh. 4:19). The LORD had not intervened on their behalf only once, when they were passing through the Red Sea. He had continued to help them overcome obstacles, as Joshua reminded them. 'The LORD your God did to the Jordan just what he had done to the Red Sea when he dried it up before us until we had crossed over. He did this so that all the peoples of the earth might know that the hand of the LORD is powerful and so that you might always fear the LORD your God' (Josh. 4:23,24).

More could have been told, but the LORD breaks off the list of his actions on their behalf to emphasise that the same response is still required, **that you may know the righteous acts of the** Lord. The purpose of this historical recital was not mere intellectual knowledge. 'Know' conveys a wider meaning. It commanded them to acknowledge and respond appropriately to what their covenant overlord had done for them. The word 'righteous' can be used to refer to either secular or religious actions, but the 'righteous acts of the Lord' are what he has done in conformity with the covenant obligations which he had taken upon himself. They are the basic factor in the relationship between the Lord and his people, and what is required from them is a response which recognises all that he has freely bestowed on them. 'We love because he first loved us' (1 John 4:19).

The Bewildered Response (6:6,7). Micah then presents us with the sort of response a typical Israelite of his day would have made to such accusations. It is unlikely that we are meant to detect here any acknowledgement of guilt on the part of the people. If that had occurred, even though accompanied by considerable spiritual ignorance, it is improbable that the judgment speech of 6:10-16 would have followed. Rather the typical reaction is one of bewilderment. 'What more can I do than I already have done to express my loyalty to the Lord?'

If the Lord has been asking his people questions, perhaps the worshipper might now on their behalf ask the Lord some. His questions are like those traditionally asked by the people as they prepared to worship the Lord (Psalm 15:1), but they no longer embody the queries of those genuinely seeking the Lord. The questions are in fact a querulous protestation that they will go to any lengths to show their devotion to him, and so are being unjustly accused. However, even as they speak in such pious tones, they expose the self-justifying spirit that permeated their worship and the gross externality of their religion.

With what shall I come before the Lord? (*verse 6*) acknowledges that the worshipper is the servant of the God of the covenant, loyally seeking to worship him in the Temple. He claims it is the mark of true piety that he comes to **bow down before the exalted God**, literally the 'God of height', an unusual expression but clearly reflecting the transcendence of God (Isa. 33:5). The worshipper does not seek to blur the difference in status that exists between him and his God. Indeed he does not approach the LORD empty handed. **Shall I come before him with burnt offerings, with calves a year old?** In the burnt offering the animal was completely consumed by fire on the altar, unlike the fellowship offering where part was returned to the worshipper to eat. It is not just any type of sacrifice that is in view, but that which is the most costly that could be made. So too with the animals used. Calves could be sacrificed from seven days old, but obviously if they had been kept and fed for a year, what the offerer was presenting was worth very much more. The typical worshipper is then protesting his willingness to present to God sacrifices of the most costly type.

He goes on to make proposals that are far-fetched, as if to suggest the unreasonable nature of the demands that the LORD was making. It also reveals the worshipper's worldly spirit. He is not aware of any reason why *he* should modify *his* behaviour, but he will bargain with God to get *him* to change. He argues, 'If it is not just a matter of the quality of our sacrifices, we will make up for it with quantity.' **Will the LORD be pleased with thousands of rams?** (*verse 7*). Solomon had made such an offering (1 Kings 8:63), but it was extremely unusual. Fairly modest amounts of oil were incorporated into the grain offerings. **Ten thousand rivers of oil** is extravagant, hyperbolic language.

He even adds, **Shall I offer my firstborn for my transgression? the fruit of my body for the sin of my soul?** It is recognised that sacrifice was appointed for their 'transgression', rebellion against their covenant overlord, and for 'sin', those actions where they had missed the mark. But their theological perception was without any personal awareness of the dimensions of their wrongdoing. They felt their piety was more than adequate, and the question seems to refer not to the child sacrifices involved in the worship of the Canaanite god Molech (2 Kings 3:27; 16:3), but to

Abraham, whose faith God tested by commanding him to sacrifice his son Isaac (Gen. 22). They were not offering to emulate the heathen, but rather claiming to be as willing as Abraham was to show their faith in God. They saw nothing wrong in their side of the relationship. Yes, God had done much for them, but they were ready and prepared to go to any lengths in their worship of him.

The Prophetic Rejoinder (6:8). 'Enough of these extravagant pretensions,' says Micah in measured tones that are in contrast with the far-fetched, almost hysterical language of the worshipper. **He has showed you** (*verse 8*). This is not necessarily a reference to God. The emphasis is not on who has done it, but on the fact that it has been done. All in the land had been informed about the terms of the covenant, so there was no need for such ludicrous speculations. **O man** serves to bring back a note of realism by pointing to man in his frailty, to cut him down to size, and to burst the bubble of his self-satisfaction, before the reality of God. **What is good** looks back to the covenant. 'Goodness' here is not something ethically abstract, nor a speculative exercise in moral philosophy. It is determined and expressed by the terms of God's covenant relationship.

What does the Lord require of you? It is the prerogative of the suzerain to make demands of his people, and so the verse is not to be understood as presenting an ethical standard in isolation from the saving work of the covenant Lord. In other words, it is not an expression of salvation by works, as if good outward behaviour on its own satisfied God and atoned for the past. Rather, it is a description of what is needed to preserve covenant fellowship. Their overlord's requirement is that those whom he has favoured with his salvation express their gratitude by living in the way he wants.

Three phrases are used to summarise the covenant requirements. The first two are essentially imitative in nature. The behaviour required is first known in, and so patterned after, what is seen in the Lord.

(1) **To act justly** goes beyond law courts that are fair. It includes

that, but requires a total life-style that accords with the standards of what the LORD has shown is right and proper, particularly by his own words and actions. 'All his ways are just, a faithful God who does no wrong' (Deut. 32:4). So those who have known how the covenant LORD behaves are to model their own behaviour towards one another on him.

(2) Mercy, or covenant loyalty, is also to characterise the response of the vassal in covenant relationship with the LORD. His overlord is the compassionate and gracious God (Exod. 34:6) who delights to show mercy (7:20). As he has personally experienced that mercy, so he is to exhibit it towards others (1 John 4:11). The second phrase, **to love mercy**, adds to the first principally the idea of willingness and delight in acting towards one's fellows with the fidelity and consideration God requires. It is not an irksome performance of an imposed duty, but a glad and spontaneous action.

(3) The third expression relates to the heavenward attitude that is to permeate covenant living. **To walk humbly** is an expression of faith. The humility involved is not some ostentatious self-effacement, but a genuine recognition of the exaltation of the sovereign LORD. 'Walk' is a Hebrew idiom for the whole of one's life, viewed as a journey. It is a walk **with your God** with whom they willingly and lovingly should travel the journey of life. To do so, they must let him choose the path that they will take, living in conscious dependence on his gracious provision.

What was being condemned was not sacrifice as appointed by God, but sacrifices as a substitute for obedience. True worship is not a matter of outer attitudes, but the inner disposition of heart and spirit (John 4:24). Those who have experienced and responded to God's love will show that in conformity to his will (John 14:23). As they reflect on the magnitude of what God has done for them in love (1 John 4:10), their inner devotion will reveal itself both in a life of obedience and in worship that magnifies God.

Micah 6:9-16: Curses of the Broken Covenant

In the previous section the LORD had called his people to account because of the emptiness of their religious practices, but still the covenant lawsuit had left the outcome of the situation open. There was scope for the people to admit the error of their ways and amend them. This section continues the theme of the LORD's dissatisfaction with his people, but now the focus is on the low public morality of the day (6:10-12), and the concluding note is the inevitability of their punishment because of their persistence in covenant breaking (6:13-16).

Listen! (*verse 9*) is a sudden cry, calling for attention. It is not the same word as is found at 6:1 to mark the beginning of the third major section of the prophecy. **The LORD is calling to the city.** 'The city' for Micah is always Jerusalem, and the LORD wants to ensure that it is listening to him. But before we are told what is said, Micah himself adds the words **and to fear your name is wisdom**. The 'fear of the LORD' indicates not an attitude of terror, but of reverent submission in awed obedience. It encapsulates the essence of the personal religious response that is enjoined in the Old Testament (Prov. 1:7). The 'name' of the LORD is not merely the sound of the word, but all that is revealed of God. Fearing his name is the response of a true follower of the LORD (Psalm 86:11). As Micah begins to tell Jerusalem what the LORD has said, he urges that they display true wisdom in their attitude to God and respond appropriately to the revelation he has given of himself and his purposes.

The message of the LORD then begins with the words: **Heed the rod and the one who has appointed it**. As the NIV footnote indicates, the meaning of the Hebrew for this line is uncertain, but 'the rod' is probably a reference to the Assyrians. When they invaded and devastated the land of Judah, they were acting as the instruments of God's righteous judgment. The same word is used in reference to them by Isaiah when God says that in their hand is the 'club of my wrath' (Isa. 10:5) and that they lifted up a 'club' against his people (Isa. 10:24). The people of Judah are called on to pay careful attention to the LORD's providential dealings with them, and to see God as the one who is really in control of the human agents he employs to carry out his purposes. In this way they will be able to interpret their experience as divine chastisement sent by the God who will not let his people go.

The LORD then specifies some of the offences that evidence their estrangement from him. Those who are satisfied with an empty religion are those whose departure from God will show itself in other areas. They thought they were placating God by their religiosity. The text of the question that is asked is also difficult to understand, but the NIV rendering **Am I still to forget?** (*verse 10*) implies they had mistaken the LORD's longsuffering for forgetfulness (Rom. 2:4). By affirming that God will certainly not forget, the rhetorical question challenges their self-contentment. He is ready to act against the **wicked house**. This unusual expression might be a distortion of the 'house of Judah' which was a way of referring to the whole nation (2 Sam. 2:4; Jer. 31:31; 33:14; Hosea 1:7).

Their **ill-gotten treasures** refers to what has been misappropriated (compare 2:2,8). One way this was done was by using **the short ephah**, which refers to the measuring basket for goods such as corn. It should have contained somewhat more than twenty litres (about five gallons). But there were no standard sizes, nor were there inspectors to assure the public that they were not being cheated by unscrupulous traders who used small measures when they weighed out goods in the market.

Such short measure was **accursed**. What God expected of his people went beyond worship in the sanctuary that outwardly conformed to his requirements. His covenant people should have ordered their lives totally in accordance with his wishes, and that extended to the every detail of their businesses and of their relationships.

The same thought is continued by another rhetorical question **Shall I acquit a man with dishonest scales, with a bag of false weights?** (*verse 11*). The expected answer is obviously 'No'. 'The dishonest scales' cheated because of the 'bag of false weights'. The weights used were stones, but their true weight would not correspond to what was marked on them: stones heavier than what was marked on them would be used to purchase commodities or weigh money, and others lighter than marked for sales or giving change. This was the all too prevalent commercial trickery of the day (Hosea 12:7; Amos 8:5). Its impact extended beyond the market place. Many would have paid rents in kind, and their value would have been underestimated if the weights used by their landlords were inaccurate. The use of such dishonest standards had been divinely proscribed (Lev. 19:35,36; Deut. 25:13-16), and it was recognised that honest scales and balances were from the LORD (Prov. 16:11; 20:23).

Her rich men (*verse 12*) refers to the royal household and the business community of Jerusalem (see on 2:1). They **are violent**, characterised by a grasping wickedness that had no respect for the rights of others (see on Jonah 3:8; Amos 5:11). They were prepared to break the law code regulating civil affairs if it was in the way of their ambitions. The implication is that this is how they had got on in the world, by treading on those they considered as obstacles. **Her people**, those who are resident in Jerusalem, **are liars and their tongues speak deceitfully**. The life of the capital had little or no respect for truth in business dealings or in ordinary living. The conduct required by the God of truth had been quite forgotten (Jer. 9:3-5).

Therefore (*verse 13*) translates a phrase which shows the LORD dissociating himself from those who behave in such a way. The action that he for his part will take will match up to what they have done. The NIV translation **I have begun to destroy you** points to the LORD's action in judgment as having already started. This involves changing the words slightly in the light of the evidence of ancient versions of Scripture. Literally, it reads 'I will make you sick, striking you', bringing you to ruin **because of your sins**.

The nature of this ruin is spelled out in 6:14,15. The curses listed remind one of passages such as Deuteronomy 28:15-68 and Leviticus 26:14-39, where the LORD details what will happen to his people if they fail to live up to his covenant standards. The curses share the characteristic of frustrating the expectations of those who have disobeyed the LORD by bringing about quite the opposite of what they had been hoping for. **You will eat but not be satisfied; your stomach will still be empty** (*verse 14*). Here again the precise meaning of the Hebrew is uncertain, but the overall thrust is clear. Famine will strike the land (Hosea 4:10; Hag. 1:6; 2:16), but it is not occasioned by natural disaster, rather by invading armies. **You will store up but save nothing, because what you save I will give to the sword.** It will be snatched from them by force.

The same theme of frustrated expectations is continued in **You will plant but not harvest; you will press olives but not use the oil on yourselves, you will crush grapes but not drink the wine** (*verse 15*). The people will not enjoy the yield of their hard work. They will be deprived of the opportunity to harvest the grain, to use the olive oil to soften their skin, or to drink the wine. Their enemies would take their produce for their own use, and the reward Israel had expected for all their hard work would elude them. They cannot expect to enjoy the fruits of the land of promise if they disobey the King who gave it to them by promise (Deut. 28:38-41).

They have been following the bad examples of the past and have not learned from past mistakes. **You have observed the statutes of Omri and all the practices of Ahab's house, and you have followed their traditions** (*verse 16*). This looks back to what had happened in the Northern Kingdom, where Omri (885-874 B.C.) had established a dynasty which had a period of success and entered into treaty relationship with the Phoenicians. Ahab (874-853 B.C.) was his better known son and heir. 'The statutes of Omri' and 'the practices of Ahab's house' are not direct references to the Baal worship that was then introduced in the North, and which subsequently infiltrated the South also. The emphasis is rather on the practical consequences of Baal worship. That religion had nothing corresponding to the ethical requirements of the covenant of the LORD but rather introduced an outlook on life which thought nothing of trampling on the rights of others. The attitude of Ahab and Jezebel towards Naboth's vineyard, where might grasps what it wants (1 Kings 21), had affected many in Judah who would have repudiated the idea that they were Baal worshippers. But their conduct was in practice moulded by that sort of thinking.

Therefore it follows as an inevitable consequence that just as the North was punished, so too the South. God cannot turn a blind eye to the misbehaviour of those who claim to be his own. **I will give you over to ruin**. This had also been an aspect of the covenant curses that the LORD had set before the people through Moses. In Deuteronomy 28:37 the word translated here as 'ruin' is rendered 'a thing of horror'. So gruesome would be the devastation that the enemy would bring on them, that others would react with revulsion when they saw the state of their land. As in Deuteronomy, there is also mentioned the ridicule to which they will be subjected. **Your people to derision; you will bear the scorn of the nations**.

Religion needs to be practical and determine what we do in all aspects of ordinary life. Paul provides the key to achieving this, 'Serve whole-heartedly, as if you were serving the Lord, not men' (Eph. 6:7), because he is the Lord of all our living. Judah's behaviour in 6:10-12 shows what happens when religion is kept in a water-tight compartment for certain situations and times, but not for business.

We are also reminded to avoid being subtly contaminated by the pressures and practices of the world around us. 'In the world', but 'not of the world' (John 17:11,14) is the pattern that the Lord sets out for his disciples. To achieve this requires constant vigilance to be sure that true righteousness and holiness determine the attitudes of our minds (Eph. 4:22,23) rather than the standards that we encounter in society.

Micah 7:1-7: Micah's Lament

Micah now tells us what it was like to live in a land that had deserted the LORD and was under his sentence of judgment. But there is more to what he has to say than just an expression of misery and grief. He also tells us in 7:7 how he sustained himself in such conditions. Rather than becoming depressed by it all, he looked to God and that enabled him to win through. This prepares the way for the triumphant conclusion of the final two sections.

He begins **What misery is mine!** (*verse 1*). This is a heart-felt cry of grief and desolation over the circumstances he has to endure (compare the cry of Baruch, Jer. 45:3). Translations vary somewhat in the way they render the compressed language of what follows, but there can be no doubt about the main point of the comparison Micah makes. **I am like one who gathers summer fruit at the gleaning of the vineyard.** It was the God-appointed custom in Israel that gleanings were left for the poor at harvest (Lev. 19:9,10; Deut. 24:19-21). Micah pictures himself as one who comes to gather fruit at harvest time but the vineyard had been harvested and gleaned. **There is no cluster of grapes to eat. None of the early figs that I crave**. He had really been wanting a nice piece of fruit, but is frustrated that everything has been removed. Figs and vines were often grown together, as the picture in 4:4 shows.

But Micah goes on to explain that it was not fruit that he had really been looking for. The vineyard corresponds to the land of Judah, and the fruit he sought were those with whom he might have like-minded fellowship in the midst of general corruption. Micah's misery over the wrongs of his day was intensified by the isolation he felt. It is a natural response of the godly to strengthen one another by associating with those who are sympathetic and will engage in a ministry of mutual encouragement (Mal. 3:16; Heb. 10:25), but the land had so largely departed from the LORD that this was not an option for Micah.

The godly have been swept from the land; not one upright man remains (*verse 2*). The 'godly' person is the one who 'loves mercy' (6:8): the words are connected. Knowing God's goodness to themselves, they respond and live up to their obligations to him and their fellows. They are conscious of living before God, and this gives an extra dimension and quality to all that they do. 'Upright' describes those who live honestly and respect their neighbours' rights. But the standard of behaviour in the land had degenerated to such an extent that none could be found (Psalm 12:1; Isa. 57:1). Compare the situation outlined in Jeremiah 5.

The prophet then describes the conduct that was prevalent in his day. It is a picture of selfish exploitation prepared to go to any lengths to achieve its goal. **All men lie in wait to shed blood.** Perhaps it is not saying all are murderers in terms of the overt act, but their attitude is such that, if carried through to its conclusion, murder would result (Prov. 12:6; Isa. 59:7). Life is a battle, and the only way to succeed is by trampling on others. **Each hunts his brother with a net**. The picture is now that of the huntsman (Psalm 57:6; Jer. 5:26) rather than the soldier or highway robber. The covenant community, which should have been a source of mutual help and support, is set at odds, each trying to get the greatest advantage for himself.

The one thing everyone is good at is being bad. **Both hands are skilled in doing evil** (*verse 3*). It is not an occasional act of wrongdoing that is being talked about, but a situation where so much wrong has been perpetrated that they have all become adept at it. **The ruler demands gifts, the judge accepts bribes, the powerful dictate what they desire**. Micah traces the social ills of his day particularly to the behaviour of administrators (see on 3:9-11). The 'ruler' is a prince, someone who ranked next to the king and was his counsellor, responsible for administration of the affairs of the kingdom. Their advice was not given on the basis of what was just, or seemed best for the land, but on which individual or pressure group had sweetened them up sufficiently. The corruption spread from the inner circles round the king to affect the judges the king had appointed. Justice was not administered impartially. It was payment of money, not being in the right, that secured a verdict in your favour. 'The powerful', literally 'the great man', covers both social standing and economic influence. They have no trouble getting what they 'desire', and the word used generally implies what is not right or acceptable. There is top-level corruption in the land. **They all conspire together**. Those in power see to it that those who are in key positions get what they want. 'Conspire' is literally 'twist', or 'weave'. The intricate contortions of their actions form a complicated background to the social degeneracy of Judah.

The best of them is like a brier, the most upright worse than a thorn hedge (*verse 4*). Micah looks at the ruling classes of his day and tries to identify those who are the best of a bad bunch either in terms of benevolence towards others, or of maintaining an honest standard of conduct. But they did not amount to very much. 'Like brier' and 'worse than a thorn hedge' perhaps continue the theme of their twisted conspiracies. They are all entangled in the existing corruption. Some may not be as grasping as others, but they will not speak out against it and rather hinder those who would contend for justice. They are an obstacle in the way that is sharp and piercing. Because they are implicated in the general way of getting things done, their actions too are harmful to others.

Then in the middle of 7:4 Micah suddenly changes his approach, and sets in opposition to their conduct the reality of God's coming intervention. What God will then do is, of course, linked to the situation he will find, and the correspondence between them is brought out by the similarity in sound and spelling of the words for 'thorn-hedge' and 'confusion'.

The day of your watchmen has come. In ancient cities the watchman played an important role, not only in patrolling the streets at night to warn of crime or fire while others slept (Song of Songs 3:3; 5:7), but also in maintaining a lookout on the city walls by day and night to warn of enemy attack. There are a number of passages where the prophets are compared to watchmen (for instance, Hosea 9:8; Jer. 6:17; Ezek. 3:17), and that seems to be the reference here. The prophets God had sent to warn the people had told them of the day when he would intervene in judgment. Micah now dramatically says it has come, perhaps in reference to the Assyrian armies surrounding Jerusalem. It could also be translated 'The day ... is coming', so confident is the prophet in anticipating the future.

The day God visits you is not the picture of a friendly gathering, but of a superior inspecting the affairs of a subordinate to ensure all is well, and to act appropriately if it is not. To show that he does not anticipate the people's conduct being approved by

God, Micah adds **Now is the time of their confusion**, (or, understanding the reference as future, 'Then will be their confusion'). They will not know what to say when the LORD exposes and scrutinises their affairs (Isa. 10:3).

Micah next reverts to exposing the decadence of society in his day. He looks now not at the top, but at the basic building blocks of personal, and particularly family, relationships. **Do not trust a neighbour; put no confidence in a friend** (*verse 5*). It is not just in the world of business or public affairs that things have gone sadly wrong. People are so out for themselves that they cannot be relied on for assistance or keeping a matter confidential. The fabric of social relationships has reached breaking point.

Matters are even worse than that. **Even with her who lies in your embrace be careful of your words**. You cannot be certain of anyone when personal advantage is the criterion of every decision. This affects even the relationship between man and wife.

The tensions thus caused in the family circle are spelled out. **For a son dishonours his father, a daughter rises up against her mother, a daughter-in-law against her mother-in-law** (*verse 6*). 'Dishonours' is literally 'thinks of as a fool', or 'calls a fool'. 'Fool' is not just referring to lack of sense, but is a term of moral depravity and spiritual insensitivity (Psalm 74:18; Isa. 32:6). The respect for elders which was vital to the cohesion of family life in Israel had gone. There is tension: indeed, warfare. **A man's enemies are the members of his own household**. These words were used in the intertestamental period to describe the social anarchy that would characterise the period before the coming of the Messianic age. Jesus also takes them up and applies them to the situation that has arisen with his coming (Matt. 10:35,36; Luke 12:53).

In the Psalms, we often find an individual telling God of all that was disturbing him, and then from the midst of his woes, there comes a sudden switch to an affirmation of faith, for example at Psalms 13:5; 31:14; 55:16. When Micah begins **But as for me** (*verse 7*), he is acting in the same way. It is not just a literary technique that he has copied from the psalms. Rather in both it is the same psychology of faith that is exhibited. Faith is not concerned with constructing a logical path from present distress to the relief that is anticipated. Instead, it affirms the reality of God's control even over the dark circumstances that surround, and trusting in him, looks expectantly for his intervention (2 Cor. 1:10; 2 Tim. 4:18).

I watch in hope for the LORD. Micah, the watchman (it is the same word as in 7:4), knows there is more to come than the threatened judgment. It is with the LORD alone that the resolution of his people's destiny lies, and therefore it is for his intervention he waits. **I wait for God my Saviour.** Waiting is an expression of personal inability to bring about progress in the situation, and an expression of God's ability to hear and help (Psalms 38:15; 130:5). The salvation that is spoken of is not only personal rescue from sin but divine deliverance from any threatening situation.

My God will hear me acknowledges God's sovereignty over events in general, and also more particularly his identification with Micah as one who had committed himself to the LORD. It is out of his personal bond in covenant with the LORD that Micah is sure his prayer will be answered (John 16:26,27). Now that the situation has been put before him, Micah is not one characterised by apathy, but by intense eagerness waiting for God to respond (Psalm 130:5-8). There is no doubt that he will.

Micah 7:8-13: Zion's Confidence

In this section Micah moves forward from the degeneracy of the nation in his own day to a time when the LORD's chastisement has already fallen on the people and they are held by the enemy in captivity. At first (7:8-10) Zion, the covenant community, is heard challenging her enemies and expressing her confidence in the LORD's intervention to deliver her from her plight. To this confidence the prophet responds with a positive declaration of the community's restoration and return (7:11-13).

We are now presented with a much changed situation and a

much changed people. The link between this section and the last is in terms of the attitude of faith. Previously it had been that of the prophet waiting for the LORD to act in times of social and religious degeneracy and apostasy. Now it is that of the repentant people waiting in faith till the LORD reverses the punishment they were undergoing. The reference in 7:10 to 'your God' has a feminine possessive in the original, and this probably resumes the feminines applied to Zion earlier (4:8). The city is viewed as representing the true people of God, and her enemies are personified in the same way in the address of 7:8.

Do not gloat over me, my enemy! (*verse 8*) shows that Micah is describing what he sees will happen when the curse of 6:16 has come into operation. The people have become the scorn and derision of the nations (4:11), but the situation is not one of total despair. They have also been brought to their senses, and now speak as those who have come to accept the prophet's warning and who realise how the LORD had been at work in their national existence. They have no quarrel with the LORD. He has acted justly. But they confidently expect that though his punishment is justified, he will reclaim his people. They are appropriating not only Micah's words of warning and condemnation, but also his message of a bright future beyond the catastrophe he had threatened. So they warn their enemies not to rejoice too soon over the downfall of the LORD's people. He has not given them up. He is using their enemies' success to teach them a lesson.

Though I have fallen, I will rise. The fall is the disaster that has overtaken the community. But just as certainly as that has occurred, so will the LORD restore a repentant Israel. **Though I sit in darkness, the LORD will be my light.** Light is associated with the felt presence of God (Psalms 27:1; 36:9). He is the one who will look favourably on his people. 'Sitting in darkness' is not a reference to death, which would rather be 'lying, or being in darkness', but rather to imprisonment (Psalm 107:10). The reference seems clearly to what Jerusalem was to suffer at the hands of the Babylonians. But the gloom will be relieved by the LORD's intervention. It is this note of confidence that pervades the closing sections of the prophecy. The LORD is the one who will intervene effectively and decisively on his people's behalf – and for this they wait in faith.

Their faith is accompanied by acknowledgement of their past failure. **Because I have sinned against him, I will bear the LORD's wrath** (*verse 9*). They are accepting that as a community they had departed from the LORD, and that consequently it was right they should 'bear the LORD's wrath', that is, the curse of the covenant they had broken. There is nothing they can say on their own behalf, but they do not anticipate that the punishment is to be without termination.

It is not the case that Zion expects to be able to do anything herself to rectify the situation that exists. She places the matter wholly in the LORD's hands, and expects the punishment to continue **until he pleads my case and establishes my right**. The case or law-suit does not seem to be a continuation of the one in chapter 6 between the LORD and his people. Now it is an action Zion is raising against her captors in that they have exceeded what God gave them permission to do when they came against her (Isa. 47:6). They had tried to destroy her, and now she seeks redress from the God of the covenant. As the oppressed party, she looks to him to advocate her cause and bring about justice for her. God as judge is a threat to those who are in the wrong, but he is the vindicator and deliverer of those who are wrongfully oppressed. Therefore Zion confidently states **He will bring me out** from the darkness of captivity and oppression **into the light** of salvation and enjoyment of his favour. **I will see his righteousness.** 'Righteousness' is used here in a way very similar to Isaiah (for example, Isa. 46:13; 51:6) and in some psalms (for example, Psalm 98:2). This is God's conduct in terms of the covenant norm he has set for himself in his dealings with his people. He has chosen them, and so he will not permit them to be badly treated but will provide them with deliverance and salvation.

Then my enemy will see it and will be covered with shame

(*verse 10*). It is Zion, the LORD's people, who continue to speak. When Zion is vindicated, it will be her oppressors' turn to blush. The charge against them is specified in terms of their mocking of Israel in her plight – and especially their mocking of Israel's God. **She who said to me, "Where is the LORD your God?"** This is the voice of defiant irreligion taunting the people and denying the existence and effective loyalty of God. It is not dissimilar to the attitude described in 4:11. When the LORD vindicates his people, **my eyes will see her downfall**. The evil power that vaunted itself against the LORD's people will be no more. **Now** is again employed to show that the future is vividly before the eyes of the speaker. (We have seen this earlier in 5:4.) **She will be trampled underfoot like mire in the streets**. This will be indeed a just fate for her spiteful and uncaring attitude.

In the final verses of this section (7:11-13), the prophet relays the LORD's endorsement of the attitude of expectation by the repentant people. He assures them that the time will come when their fortunes will be restored. **The day for building your walls will come** (*verse 11*) may possibly refer to re-erecting the walls of Zion that were demolished when the city was captured. But it is not the usual word for a city-wall that is employed. It is rather that for a stone fence, and the reference is probably to the setting up again of stone walls throughout the rural community. It goes further. **It will be the day for extending your boundaries** from the smaller confines of the Judean kingdom back to the extensive territory held in David and Solomon's day, even the boundaries promised by the LORD (Gen. 15:18-21; 1 Kings 4:21).

When we read these words, we are inevitably led to ask if and when all this has been accomplished. To a certain extent we can see it coming true in the return from the captivity (Ezra 1:1-4). But Judah's fortunes were never restored to the extent that their original boundaries were regained. The prophecy awaits fulfilment on a grander scale, and this is associated with the rule of the Messianic king (Psalms 2:8; 72:8). At present the boundaries of his kingdom are being extended by his church as it fulfils the Commission he gave it (Matt. 28:19,20; Luke 24:47). The role of Zion has been taken over by the heavenly Jerusalem (Heb. 12:22), and this awaits the final consummation of the new Jerusalem (Rev. 21,22) in which all the promises of restoration given to God's people find their ultimate realisation in the presence of their King.

The picture of 7:12 continues to teach the people of Micah's day of the LORD's restoration in terms of images they would understand. **In that day** (*verse 12*) links the happenings of this verse to the revival of Zion's fortunes just described. It may imply that the restoration is to be accomplished by the return of the exiles from the places where they had been taken captive and where they had fled to seek safety. Alternatively, the description here may parallel that of 4:1,2, and **people will come to you** refers to those who have turned to the LORD from among the nations. **From Assyria and the cities of Egypt, even from Egypt to the Euphrates and from sea to sea and from mountain to mountain**. 'From sea to sea' is from the Mediterranean Sea through to the Persian Gulf, and 'from mountain to mountain', though a less common expression, seems to correspond to the area from the mountains in the north of Mesopotamia through to Sinai. But it is not the precise geographical area that matters. It is a picture of the extensive area covered by the realm of the LORD.

As well as the restoration of his people's fortunes, and the gathering of the nations to them, Micah presents a third element in the LORD's intervention on behalf of his own. He will judge those who remain apart from him and his loyal subjects. **The earth will become desolate because of its inhabitants, as the result of their deeds** (*verse 13*). The earth is here obviously with the exception of Israel's restored territory. Elsewhere in the day of the LORD's intervention on behalf of his own there will be experienced the destroying force of his anger. It is not capricious. What he does will be a warranted reaction to the misdeeds of the peoples of the earth (2 Thess. 1:9,10).

Micah 7:14-20: Grace and Truth

Micah ends his prophecy on a note of confident expectation based on the promised gracious deliverance of the LORD. With the exception of 7:15 where the LORD responds to the petitions of his believing people, Micah throughout this section gives voice to their prayers and praise. The day of deliverance has not in fact arrived, but the LORD in whom they trust has committed himself. Faith, confessing the character and power of the LORD, finds in his word a more than sufficient guarantee that his salvation will come.

7:14,15 are to be understood as a prayer of the people and the response of the LORD to their petition. The people ask on their own behalf, **Shepherd your people with your staff, the flock of your inheritance** (*verse 14*). The shepherd was the ruler and provider. In Micah's prophecy this way of viewing the LORD's activity provides a unifying theme, being found in the three sections of hope (see also 2:12; 5:4). The people are his 'flock' (Psalms 74:1; 80:1; 95:7; 100:3). They are pleading the promises of the covenant by which they had become 'your people' (Exod. 6:7) and 'your inheritance' (Deut. 4:20; 9:26,29), the people God had chosen for his own. Though now, as a consequence of their spiritual rebellion against their God, they are not enjoying the privileges which ought to be theirs, in repentance they plead not what they are in themselves, but what God had divinely constituted them to be. They look to their Shepherd to deal with them graciously.

It is difficult to be sure how the description the people give of themselves ought to be understood. **Which lives by itself in a forest, in fertile pasturelands** may well combine two elements of earlier prophecies. 'By itself' ('solitarily' AV) looks back to the ancient prophecy of Balaam about 'a people who live apart' (Num. 23:9), which was taken up again by Moses in his final blessing on Israel when he said they 'will live in safety alone' (Deut. 33:28). There is also reference to the bounty of the land that the LORD had provided for his people (Exod. 3:8; Deut. 6:10,11). If so, the people are anticipating a return to the ideal conditions they will enjoy as benefits of the divine shepherding.

But the word 'forest' is the same as that rendered 'thickets' in 3:12. That may point to the people speaking of a time when the conditions envisaged there have been realised, that is, the devastation of the LORD's judgment. Certainly, their words do seem intended to describe their circumstances as they speak. The ruined state of the Temple Mount, indeed of the whole land, has come as promised. 'In fertile pasturelands' is literally 'in the middle of a fruitful field'. The situation presented may be one where the much more fertile land lower down is under enemy control, and those of the people who are left in the land (for not all were taken into captivity) have been reduced to living in isolated circumstances in the less productive forest and mountain areas. It would then be on the basis of their present deprivation that they plead with God.

Let them feed in Bashan and Gilead as in days long ago. Bashan lay to the north and west of the Sea of Galilee, and was an area of considerable fertility. Gilead is a less well defined area on the west bank of the Jordan to the south of Bashan (see Map II). While more rugged, it was still a very productive area (Numbers 32:1). These Transjordan territories had been occupied at the time of the Conquest, but lost since. This request looks back to the time of the settlement in the land, and probably also to the time of the Empire under David and Solomon, and asks in terms of the promise given of the former dominion being restored (4:8) that the people would enjoy what was promised in the covenant.

Micah then cites the words of the LORD's response to the prayer. The answer re-introduces the theme of the Exodus, already found at 4:10 and 6:4, and this continues to underlie the rest of the prophecy. **As in the days when you came out of Egypt, I will show them my wonders** (*verse 15*). The Exodus functioned in the thinking of the Old Testament church much the same way as the Cross does for the church now. It was the model by which they were taught about the LORD's saving intervention on behalf of his people. He now promises them that he will again intervene as dramatically and effectively on their behalf. His 'wonders' are his acts of power which bring about the redemption of his people (Exod. 3:20; Psalm

78:32). They are beyond human ability and cause astonishment when they occur.

In 7:16,17 we again hear the prophet present the response of the believing people. Encouraged by the reference to an Exodus style display of God's power, they remember how the nations were then devastated before Israel (Psalm 136:10-22), and expect that those who were now oppressing them will be similarly treated. **Nations will see** (*verse 16*) what God has done for his people and **be ashamed**, referring back to 7:10. Completely **deprived of all their power** in the face of the might of God, **they will lay their hands on their mouths**. This was a traditional expression of surprised shock and wonder (Job 21:5; 29:9). **Their ears will become deaf** continues the picture of their consternation at the reversal of the fortunes of Israel. The news that reaches them is such that they will refuse to listen to it.

The enemies of the people of God will experience utter humiliation. **They will lick dust like a snake, like creatures that crawl on the ground** (*verse 17*). Licking the dust was often used to express abject defeat, and prostration before a superior (Psalm 72:9; Isa. 49:23). **They will come trembling out of their dens** so shaken will they be by what God has shown in his power. **They will turn in fear to the LORD our God, and will be afraid of you**. The use of 'fear' here might indicate that the display of God's saving power has brought the nations to their senses and so they turn in reverence to the LORD. But probably the use of 'our God' rather than 'their God' indicates it is only the reaction of terror that is in view.

In 7:18-20 there is praise for the incomparable God. Micah's name means 'Who is like the LORD?' and there is obvious allusion to it here in **Who is a God like you?** (*verse 18*). Such a question was a traditional device to indicate the supremacy and uniqueness of the one true God. It picks up the theme of the Exodus from 7:15 by echoing the question Moses asked in his victory song after the people had passed through the Red Sea, 'Who among the gods is like you, O LORD?' (Exod. 15:11).

But now in a very significant prophetic presentation of the

spiritual significance of the Exodus, the emphasis turns from the liberation the LORD has granted his people from their enemies (7:15), to the even greater wonder of the liberation he grants them from the effects of their own sin. **Who pardons sin and forgives the transgression of the remnant of his inheritance** looks back to similar words in Exodus 34:6,7 where, after the incident of the Golden Calf, the people are restored because of the LORD's gracious pardon. The mention of 'the remnant' brings a shadow of judgment into the picture (2:12). His people have a history which is not all to their credit. But the focus is on the consummation of the promise to those who remain and are taken by the LORD as his own.

'Sin' (deviation from the right standard), 'transgression' (rebellion against a superior), and in 7:19 'iniquity' (missing the target) are three basic Old Testament words to describe the wrong that Israel had committed against her God. The occurrence of these three words intensifies the evil of their past conduct and throws into greater prominence the unmerited graciousness of God. The extent of his saving action is also brought out by the words that are employed to describe his mercy. He 'pardons' by lifting up the burden of their guilt that was crushing them, and carrying it away. He 'forgives' by overlooking their offences, and passing on to another matter.

You do not stay angry for ever but delight to show mercy. God's anger at his people's sin is justified, but his fatherly chastisement of them is not continued indefinitely (Psalm 103:9; Isa. 57:16). It gives him far greater satisfaction to extend 'mercy', which refers to what the LORD does over and above any claim that could be made upon him. It is his gracious pleasure to take back into his favour those who have wandered and strayed.

You will again have compassion on us (*verse 19*) speaks of the deep and tender love which the LORD displays towards his children (Psalm 103:13). That had not changed. He had acted as a father to chastise his people when they wandered from him and refused to repent (Heb. 12:5-7). But now they look forward to entering into full and unrestricted enjoyment of the blessings of that love in recovered fellowship with him.

You will tread our sins underfoot. Their sin had been a hostile power acting against the LORD, but he will subdue it and render them subservient to his purposes. He is the Victor who crushes his people's sin and ensures that it is no longer their master (Rom. 6:17).

The people also describe the day when God will **hurl all our iniquities into the depths of the sea**. Micah here uses a vivid comparison drawn from the experience of the Exodus. Then the LORD had hurled Pharaoh's chariots and his army into the sea, and they had sunk to the depths like a stone and like lead in the mighty waters (Exod. 15:4,5,10). Now the enemy is the people's own wrongdoing, and in the renewal of the Exodus experience their sin will undergo the same fate at the LORD's hands. The Egyptians were prevented from catching up with the fleeing Israelites and reversing their deliverance. The freedom of the people of God will not be marred by some consequence of their past sin catching up with them to spoil their delight in the provision God has made for them. Just as not one of the entire army of Pharaoh that followed the Israelites into the Red Sea survived (Exod. 14:28), so too the consequences of 'all' their iniquities will be swept away by God.

Great though the Exodus had been in the history of God's people, there is an even greater wonder still to be found in God's gracious pardoning of his people and in the completeness with which the covenant God deals with sin and obliterates it from the lives and records of his people.

He does this because of his covenant commitment to them, or rather to their forefathers, to whom he had sworn in the past (Gen. 12:2,3; Psalm 105:9,10). **You will be true to Jacob, and show mercy to Abraham, as you pledged on oath to our fathers in days long ago** (*verse 20*). Truth and mercy are paired as descriptive of God's commitment to his covenant (Psalm 85:10, AV), and of what should characterise his people's response. Truth represents reliability. It is the consistency with which God can be counted on to measure up completely to all that he has committed himself to. His 'mercy' or 'steadfast love' (7:18) reflects the extent to which he maintains all that is involved in the relationship with his people, no matter how forgetful they may have become. It is often translated by the word 'grace', reflected in the grace and truth that came through Jesus Christ (John 1:17). No matter how much time has passed since the pledge was given, his word and oath are 'two unchangeable things in which it is impossible for God to lie' (Heb. 6:18) and so faith is greatly encouraged. The affirmation of the divine promise is made sure in Christ (2 Cor. 1:20).

Study Guide

Micah 1:1-7

verse 2: Notice how important hearing and listening are when the word of God is spoken. What sort of hearing is not really hearing at all? (Matthew 15:10; Mark 4:9-12; Luke 8:18; Revelation 3:6)

verse 4: How useful is it to approach spiritual matters indirectly? (2 Samuel 12:1-14; Psalm 50; Amos 1,2; Acts 17:16-33)

verses 5 and 6: What precautions should we observe in trying to learn from what has happened to others? (Luke 13:1-5; Philemon 15)

Micah 1:8-16

verse 8:   What function does showing oneself to be affected by the situation of the impenitent have in presenting the gospel to them? (Jeremiah 9:1; Luke 13:34,35; Romans 9:2; 2 Corinthians 11:29)

verse 10: Why would Micah find the attitude of the LORD's enemies a critical feature of the coming judgment upon his people? (Psalms 25:2; 35:25; 42:10; 89:50; 119:94,95. See also comments on 4:11.)

Micah 2:1-11

verse 1: What dangers does Scripture associate with wealth and material prosperity? (Deuteronomy 8:17; Job 31:24-25, 28; Psalms 49:6,7; 52:7; Ecclesiastes 4:8; Luke 8:14; Revelation 3:17)

What attitude should be adopted towards wealth and possessions? (Proverbs 3:9,10; Matthew 25:27; 1 Corinthians 16:2; 2 Corinthians 8:2)

How may power be misused? (Luke 3:12-14; 19:8; James 5:1-6)

verse 2: What are the consequences of coveting? (Psalm 39:6; Proverbs 1:18,19; Ephesians 5:5) How may we guard against them? (Matthew 6:33; Philippians 4:10-13; James 4:2)

verse 6: How may we test the claims of those who say they are bringing the word of God? (Deuteronomy 13:1-5; 18:17-22; Matthew 7:15-23; 2 Timothy 3:8; 4:3,4)

Micah 2:12,13

verse 12: Scripture frequently compares the relationship between God and his people to that between a shepherd and his flock. What do Ezekiel 34 and John 10:1-21 tell us about this relationship?

verse 13: In what ways does the salvation of God break through the hostile forces that surround his people? (Isaiah 42:7,13; 59:16-21; 61:1-7; 1 Corinthians 15:21-26; Hebrews 2:9-15)

Micah 3:1-12

verse 1: Those who speak on behalf of the Lord are directed to do so without consideration of the social or political status of those whom they address. What other instances can you find of fearless proclamation of what God wants to be known? (1 Kings 17:1; Matthew 14:4; Acts 4:13,18-20,31; Galatians 2:6,11)

verse 4: See Study Guide: Jonah, 1:6.

verse 8: There are many Old Testament passages which record God's Spirit coming upon individuals (for instance, Exodus 31:3; Numbers 11:17; 27:18; Judges 6:34; 1 Samuel 10:6; 1 Chronicles 12:18; 28:12). What did this signify? Is it different from the way the Spirit is given in the New Testament? (Luke 24:49; Acts 1:8; 2:4; Ephesians 3:16)

verse 11: What causes people to have a false sense of security as regards their future destiny? (Genesis 11:4; Isaiah 28:14-19; 30:1-5; Romans 2:3-4,17-27; Galatians 6:7,8; 1 Thessalonians 5:3)

Micah 4:1-8

verse 1: Future glory is revealed to encourage the faithful to persevere. What significance may prophecy of the future have for the unrepentant? (Ezekiel 43:10-12)

How does the New Testament show the international aspect of this prophecy already becoming true? (Matthew 28; Acts 13:47; Romans 15:19; Revelation 5:9)

verse 2: How does Christ act as judge? (Isaiah 9:7; 11:3-5; 42:1; Matthew 25:31,32; John 5:22-29; Acts 17:31)

verse 3: In what way should the absence of strife characterise the

Christian church? (Isaiah 32:16,17; Matthew 5:9; Romans 14:19; 15:13; 1 Corinthians 14:33; Ephesians 4:3; Hebrews 12:14)

verse 8: When did her king come to Zion? (Matthew 21:5; John 12:15; Revelation 17:14; 19:16)

Micah 4:9-13

verse 9: What does Scripture teach us about relying on man? (Psalms 62:9; 118:8,9; 146:3; Isaiah 2:22; 31:3; Jeremiah 17:5,6; John 2:24,25)

verse 10: What is the significance of 'redemption'? (Leviticus 25:25-34; Ruth 3:9; 4:4,6; Acts 20:28; Galatians 3:13; 1 Peter 1:10,11)

verse 12: What does Scripture teach about the plans of God? (Psalms 40:5; 77:19; Isaiah 55:8,9; Matthew 11:25; Romans 11:33-36)

Micah 5:1-6

verse 2: What does Scripture teach regarding the pre-existence of the Messiah? (Isaiah 9:6; John 1:1,2; 8:58; 17:5,24; Colossians 1:15-19; Hebrews 1:10)

verse 3: Show how important unity is as a feature of the Messianic kingdom. (Psalm 133:1; Isaiah 11:12,13; Jeremiah 3:18; 32:39; 50:4; Ezekiel 37:15-23; Hosea 1:11; Romans 12:4,5; 1 Corinthians 12:12,13; Ephesians 2:14-18; 4:3-6)

verse 4: How significant a part of salvation is the security that is bestowed by Christ? (Leviticus 26:5,6; Psalm 102:27,28; John 10:28; 17:12; 1 Peter 1:5)

verse 5: How does peace come from Christ? (Isaiah 9:6; Luke 2:14; John 14:27; Ephesians 2:17)

Micah 5:7-15

verse 7: What role is assigned to the people of God when they know his salvation? (Zechariah 8:13; Matthew 5:14; Galatians 6:9,10; Philippians 2:15,16)

verse 8: How do we know that the people of God will enjoy

victory over all opposition? (Isaiah 25:8; Romans 8:37-39; 1 John 4:4; 5:5; Jude 24; Revelation 7:9,10)

verses 9-14: In what ways are the LORD's people purified? (Romans 6:6,11; 13:14; Colossians 3:5)

verse 15: Is it right to punish the ignorant? (2 Thessalonians 1:8; Luke 12:47,48; John 15:22; Romans 2:12-16; 3:9-18; 1 Timothy 1:13; James 3:1)

Micah 6:1-8

verse 1: Is 'covenant' a significant feature of New Testament teaching? (Matthew 26:28; Luke 1:72; 2 Corinthians 3:6; Hebrews 7:22; 8:6-13; 12:24; 13:20)

verse 5: The requirement 'to remember' is a key factor at all times. What should we be remembering now? (Matthew 16:9; 1 Corinthians 11:24,25; Ephesians 2:11; 1 Thessalonians 1:3; 2:9; 2 Timothy 2:8; Hebrews 10:32; 13:3,7)

verse 6: What types of offering are required of the New Testament church? (Hosea 14:2; Romans 6:19; 12:1; Hebrews 13:15,16)

verse 8: What part should humility play in Christian conduct? (Matthew 11:29; Colossians 2:18-23; 3:12; James 4:10; 1 Peter 5:5,6)

Micah 6:9-12

verse 9: Why should we always be ready to pay careful attention to God's rebuke? (Deuteronomy 8:5; Job 5:17; Haggai 1:5-11; 1 Corinthians 11:32; Revelation 3:19,20)

verse 11: False balances are forbidden both in the Old Testament and in the New Testament (Leviticus 19:35,36; Proverbs 11:1; Matthew 7:12; Philippians 4:8). To what other business practices may a similar ban be extended?

verse 12: Speech is a very important aspect of Christian conduct. What guidelines exist as to how we should speak? (Proverbs 12:17,22; 21:6; 29:20; Isaiah 59:4; Zechariah 8:16-17; John 8:44; Ephesians 4:15,25-27,29-31; Colossians 3:9; 1 Timothy 1:10)

Micah 7:1-7

verse 1: What role should mutual encouragement play in difficult circumstances? (1 Samuel 23:16; Malachi 3:16; 1 Thessalonians 5:11; Hebrews 3:13; 10:24,25)

verse 6: What should characterise family relationships? (Proverbs 6:20; Ephesians 5:22-6:3; Colossians 3:18-21; 1 Peter 3:1-7)

verse 7: How should faith react to perplexing occurrences? (Job 13:15; 2 Chronicles 20:12-15)

Micah 7:8-13

verse 9: When faith acknowledges the rightness of the LORD's chastisement, how does it react? (1 Samuel 3:18; Lamentations 3:29; Hebrews 12:11)

Micah 7:14-20

verse 18: How should we praise God for his gracious intervention? (Deuteronomy 33:26; 1 Kings 8:23; Psalms 35:10; 86:5; Daniel 9:9)

verse 19: What action does the LORD take with his people's sin? (Deuteronomy 30:6; Psalm 103:12; Isaiah 38:17; Jeremiah 50:20; Ezekiel 11:19; 36:25; Hosea 14:4; Romans 6:18; 8:2)

verse 20: What is true of the LORD's promises? (Luke 1:54, 55, 72-74; Romans 15:8,9; Hebrews 6:18)

Nahum

Overview

If a book of just forty-seven verses foretelling the destruction of an ancient city thousands of years ago is not to escape being quickly passed over, it must be shown to be relevant. That it is written in vigorous and dramatic language which equals anything in the rest of the Old Testament does not help much, because the descriptions are of war, death and crushing ruin. What have they to do with the revelation of God's grace? The emphasis on God's wrath and vengeance increases our unease. And the criticism frequently goes further. Nahum says nothing, it is alleged, about the faults of Judah. He rather gloats in a jingoistic fashion over what is to befall Assyria. Many have indeed gone so far as to exclaim that what we hear in Nahum is virtually the voice of the false prophets such as those who opposed Micah and Jeremiah – intensely nationalistic, down on their enemies, sure of their own future and blind to their own faults. That, however, is an inadequate and quite erroneous assessment of Nahum.

The relevance of Nahum begins to emerge when we consider the circumstances of the prophecy. In moving on from the book of Micah to that of Nahum, we have come forward by about fifty years, but the national and international scene is still dominated by the might of Assyria. The emphasis, however, has changed. In Micah, Assyria was the rod the LORD had appointed to chastise his wayward people (Micah 6:9). Now, the stress is on the cruelty with which Assyria carried out this task, overstepping what God permitted, as Isaiah had prophesied she would (Isa. 10:5-7). This is a message directed at the agony of the people of God as they suffer at the hands of a barbarous regime. It claims our attention because of what it tells us about God and his attitude towards such behaviour. Just as much as in Micah's prophecy, we are being asked to exclaim 'Who is like the LORD?'

The world is still polluted with evil. Successive generations continue to provide examples of regimes that act with barbarous cruelty. Platitudes provide no remedy for those who are suffering in such situations, or for those who are compelled to look on helplessly. It is not easy to respond to the anguished query, 'How can there really be a God who allows all this to happen?' But faith's first step is to lay hold of the truth that God does rule over 'the world and all who live in it' (1:5).

The LORD is also implacably opposed to evil. 'I am against you' (2:13; 3:5). He will display his justice and power by bringing all that is opposed to him and his people to an end. The collapse of Nineveh is an outstanding example of how the empires of man may seem outwardly impregnable, and yet when the LORD decrees, their end comes swiftly.

We are also presented with the truth that the LORD's judgment on evil is linked with his purposes of grace (1:7,8; see also on 1:12-2:2). When he intervenes in judgment, there is inevitably a dual impact. To establish the righteous is to overthrow their enemies. 'Your kingdom come' is a two-edged prayer. The overthrow of Nineveh reveals the pattern common to every divine action against the kingdom of darkness, and so it foreshadows the final extirpation of evil from the LORD's domains when he brings his people into the heavenly kingdom in the consummation (Rev. 22:14,15). As Paul said, 'God is just: He will pay back trouble to those who trouble you and give relief to you who are troubled, and to us as well. This will happen when the Lord Jesus is revealed from heaven in blazing fire with his powerful angels. He will punish those who do not know God and do not obey the gospel of our Lord Jesus. They will be punished with everlasting destruction and shut out from the presence of the Lord and from the majesty of his power on the day he comes to be glorified in his holy people and to be marvelled at among all those who have believed' (2 Thess. 1:6-10).

Nahum 1:1: The Capital of the Empire

An oracle concerning Nineveh (*verse 1*). 'Oracle' indicates that this is a message given by God. But it has always been a problem to know just how to translate the word. Many would still prefer the translation 'burden', as in the AV. It is generally used of an ominous message, one of disaster and impending calamity (Isa. 13:1; 14:28; 21:1). It is the sort of message that would be like a weight tied round the neck of the place or country named, and would act as a load pulling it down to its doom. Certainly that is true of the message that Nahum here relays.

How we assess what the original impact of the title was depends very much on when we date the prophecy. Accepting it as a true prophecy, and not as something written up afterwards to look like a prediction, it must obviously have been written before Nineveh fell in 612 B.C. Nahum also mentions the capture of Thebes in Upper Egypt as something that has already happened (3:8) – and that took place in 663 B.C. Opinions differ as to precisely when in the interval Nahum delivered this prophecy. Some, wanting him to be little better than an informed and astute political commentator, would date it only a short time before 612. Others argue that, while Nahum was well informed about the sack of Thebes, there is no indication that he is aware of its recovery by the Egyptians in 654 B.C., and so would place it before that. Certainly, I think we must date the prophecy earlier than 635 B.C. when the power of the Assyrians began to decline. 1:13 implies Judah was still oppressed by the Assyrians, and that does not fit in with the reign of King Josiah (640-609 B.C.) when the pressure of Assyria was removed, but with the reign of Manasseh (686-642 B.C.), who paid tribute to Assyria and was even deported for a time by the Assyrians to Babylon (2 Chron. 33:11). Against that background Nahum's news that he had a message of impending disaster for Nineveh would have been a startling, almost unbelievable, revelation.

Nineveh was the capital of Assyria in Nahum's day, and was thus at the centre of a vast empire, which was at the height of its power. It was a city with a long history, being mentioned as early as Genesis 10. It had been, however, only one of the many royal cities of Assyria till Sennacherib (705-681 B.C.) made it his capital at the end of the 8th century B.C., i.e. around 700 B.C. He spent most of his twenty-five year reign enlarging and strengthening the old city. The former palace was pulled down, and a vast new one built. Its remains have not yet been fully excavated, but its large rooms and spacious halls are easily traced. Sennacherib called it 'The Palace Without a Rival'. He provided the city with new temples, broad streets, and public parks. There was also a massive aqueduct bringing water into it from the mountains to the east. A double rampart encircled the city for the protection of its perhaps 300,000 inhabitants, and an armoury covering 16 hectares (40 acres). Of the cities of the ancient world only Babylon would be larger.

What is more, Sennacherib was followed by two kings who also enhanced the city, each building another grand palace: Esarhaddon (681-669) and Ashurbanipal (669-626). Their empire stretched from Egypt through Palestine and Syria, into much of Asia Minor, and down through Mesopotamia to the Persian Gulf – and Nineveh was the focus of its power and wealth. The Assyrian kings used much of the tribute and booty that poured in from many nations to fortify and enhance their capital.

Yet here is 'the burden of Nineveh': a message of impending doom. How incredible to an empire at the height of its success! Yet with what relief it would have been heard by those who were among its subject nations. Judah had already lived through almost a century of Assyrian terror and ruthlessness, and her circumstances were not exceptional. This was no benevolent regime. The Assyrians made no secret of the blood and torture by which they maintained control over their subjects. They used calculated cruelty as an instrument to repress opposition. The records they have left spanning two and a half centuries tell the same tale throughout. In terms of atrocities perpetrated, the Assyrian empire has to be ranked with the concentration camps of Nazi Germany, the Cambodia of the Khmer Rouge and Pol Pot and the Uganda of Idi Amin – once we start to list them, there are uncomfortably many. Assyria is but one instance of what happens when lust for power is combined with callous indifference to human suffering.

There is also a second part to the title. **The book of the vision of Nahum the Elkoshite**. Only here does 'book' occur in the title of a prophecy. We need not necessarily conclude that Nahum did not speak to the people of his day, but remembering that it was the reign of Manasseh the persecutor, his prophecy may well have been written down from the first. The book certainly shows that it was carefully composed.

It is also significant that it is called a 'vision'. Nahum recorded what would otherwise have been unknown, not because he was more gifted, or better informed than others in his day, but because God had permitted him to see what would happen. It is this revelation that he transmits, and in calling it a 'vision' he places himself in the ranks of the prophets, and claims divine authority for what he has to relate.

The name 'Nahum' is only found here in the Old Testament, though we know from archaeological remains that it was in fact fairly common. It probably means 'full of comfort', or is a short form of the name 'the LORD is full of comfort', and as such connected with the name Nehemiah.

He is not called a prophet, though 'burden' and 'vision' make that claim implicitly. 'The Elkoshite' identifies his home town as Elkosh, which might have been somewhere in Galilee, or more probably another site 32 kilometres south west of Jerusalem, which would put him as coming from the same general area as Micah (see Map II). As we shall see, he shows considerable familiarity with the prophecies of Isaiah, citing them on a number of occasions, and it is speculative, but by no means impossible, that he was one of the disciples of Isaiah (Isa. 8:16).

Nahum 1:2-6: The LORD of the Covenant

Nahum lived in bleak times. Judah was under the heel of Assyria, and the king of Judah was Manasseh, of whom it is recorded that he led the people astray, 'so that they did more evil than the nations the LORD had destroyed before the Israelites' (2 Kings 21:9). In the face of national apostasy and persecution by the civil power, it would have been no wonder to those remaining loyal to the LORD that he had raised up Assyria to oppress the land. It was after all a just judgment for their national sins.

But there was more to it than national oppression as a result of national apostasy. The hideous cruelty of the oppressor far surpassed in enormity anything that had been perpetrated by Judah. Would this proud and cruel nation be allowed to get off with her atrocities? Her empire was vast; her power unchallenged; the nations were terrorised before her. How could she be stopped?

Nahum provides the response of faith. No matter how ominous the problem, faith resolutely refuses to view matters horizontally, looking only to man and what he can do to resolve the problem. Nahum does not talk about armed resistance, guerrilla fighting, or political intrigue. Instead he begins with a declaration of faith. He looks heavenward. He looks to God, and asserts in the perspective of what God is, what will happen to Nineveh.

But it is not the reality of God in general that Nahum focuses on. It is rather God as he has been pleased to enter into relationship with his people. By sheer repetition of the name, 'the LORD', Nahum emphasises his point. The NIV, in common with many English translations, uses 'LORD' with small capitals to represent the covenant name of God, Jehovah, or Yahweh, which is generally reckoned to be a more accurate pronunciation of it. It occurs three times in 1:2, and ten times in the first chapter. He is the one to focus on. He is the one who has to be taken into account in any final reckoning.

In contrast to the repetition of the name of the LORD, apart from 1:1, the name of Nineveh is not mentioned in chapter 1. It occurs only once in chapter 2 (2:8), and once in chapter 3 (3:7), and Assyria is named only in 3:18. If it were not for the title in 1:1, we would not at first be sure about the identity of the enemies Nahum talks about. The NIV does introduce the name of Nineveh quite often in underbrackets (for instance, in 1:8, 11, 14), but Nahum deliberately did not. He would not put her on a par with the LORD. In that perspective Nineveh is a nameless nobody. And, of course, Nahum was right. Who cares about Nineveh now?

But the truths Nahum expresses about the LORD are still valid – and alas (!) needed in a world where evil empires arise and men pitilessly butcher and terrorise one another. The strength of faith lies in being able to grasp that the seemingly unassailable Ninevehs of this world have to reckon with the reality of the LORD.

Nahum declares that **the LORD is a jealous and avenging God** (*verse 2*). The covenant LORD will deal decisively with all those who rise up to disrupt the bond he has created between himself and his people. We have, however, to be careful as to how we understand the idea of 'a jealous God'. Jealousy as expressed by sinful people is usually a corrupting, evil influence born of unjustified suspicion and personal insecurity. But in essence it is a vigilant commitment to maintain a relationship. The description of God as 'jealous' reflects the intensity of his love and of his determination to maintain the commitment between himself and his people. One implication of this is that his people must in turn devote themselves exclusively to him. He will permit no rival for their obedience and affections. 'Be careful not to forget the covenant of the LORD your God that he made with you; do not make for yourselves an idol in the form of anything the LORD your God has forbidden. For the LORD your God is a consuming fire, a jealous God' (Deut. 4:23,24).

Nahum also speaks of the LORD as being an 'avenging God', and goes on to say **the LORD takes vengeance and is filled with wrath. The LORD takes vengeance on his foes**. Three times he emphasises that the LORD is the one who takes vengeance (see on Micah 5:15). Again that is easily misunderstood in terms of the blood feuds and petty malice that human squabbling often engenders. This vengeance, however, is not private retaliation, but the assertion of the sovereign rights of the LORD (Psalm 94:1). It is not vindictiveness, but vindication. The LORD clears his reputation for justice and righteousness over against those who would trample his requirements underfoot (Isa. 59:18). It is the exercise of due authority by one whose authority has been impugned. 'El', the word used here for God, emphasises his power, and so when he acts, those who oppose him will be unable to mount a successful response.

The LORD's vengeance is the corollary of his jealousy, for it not only requires his people to be single-minded in their devotion to him, it also means that he will not permit any third party to disrupt the relationship between himself and his people (Deut. 32:41-43). Notice how in the second part of 1:2 Nahum speaks of 'his' foes and 'his' enemies. They were Judah's enemies in the first place. This is an indication of the identification of interest between the LORD and his people.

He is also the LORD who is 'filled with wrath', that is, literally 'master or lord of wrath', possessing wrath. It is a word of intense and passionate feeling. God is not lukewarm about anyone or anything that mars the relationship he has created. Despite appearances, the Judge of all the earth has not shrugged off the infringements of his law as minor matters of little consequence. He has judicially determined to act against those who have pitted their puny might against him. He **maintains his wrath against his enemies**. It might appear that one act after another is perpetrated with impunity, but God is watching and he is waiting – and when he is ready, he will act.

Nahum then develops his argument against those who would say, 'Look at all that is happening. Why has God not acted sooner if he could?' In response to such an objection, Nahum points back to the covenant revelation of God. **The LORD is slow to anger and great in power; the LORD will not leave the guilty unpunished** (*verse 3*). Remember how he proclaimed his name and set out his character, 'The LORD, the LORD, the compassionate and gracious God, slow to anger, abounding in love and faithfulness, maintaining love to thousands, and forgiving wickedness, rebellion, and sin. Yet he does not leave the guilty unpunished; he punishes the children and their children for the sin of the fathers to the third and fourth generation' (Exod. 34:6,7).

God's justice is not impaired because of the apparent delay. It is because he is 'great in power' that he can let matters run on for so long, and they do not get out of his control. He does not act with the swift response of human anger, but with the deliberateness of the merciful and gracious God. Remember how he sent Jonah to that great city Nineveh with the call to repentance (Jonah 3:4,5).

In the second part of 1:3 and in 1:4,5, Nahum emphasises God's power. He uses graphic images, some of them generalised from the experience of God's people at the Exodus, and at the crossing of the river Jordan. His point is that if God can do this in the natural realm, can he not also act against the empires and united forces of man?

His way is in the whirlwind and the storm. The whirlwind and the storm are chosen to represent the suddenness of God's action (Psalm 18:7-15; Isa. 66:15; 1 Thess. 5:3) and the devastating effect of his power. **Clouds are the dust of his feet**. That does not seem to be a reference to a theophany as when God came to Mount Sinai enveloped in a cloud (Exod. 19:16). Clouds are often associated with the coming of deity to emphasise heavenly grandeur (Psalm 104:3; Rev. 1:7). But here the picture is developed from an army hurrying to battle, and kicking up dust with their boots. When God comes to act, so great is the power of his presence that clouds are what he stirs up.

The command of the Creator is sufficient to change the order of nature. **He rebukes the sea and dries it up; he makes all the rivers run dry** (*verse 4*). He is the one whose mere rebuke (Isa. 50:2) dries up the sea, which was viewed in the Ancient World as a hostile deity. The language reminds one of descriptions of the Exodus (Isa. 51:10), and also of the crossing of the river Jordan (Psalm 114:3-5). **Bashan and Carmel wither and the blossoms of Lebanon fade**. Bashan, on the east of the Jordan (see on Micah 7:14, and Map II), was noted for its rich pasture land and herds of cattle. Carmel was a fertile mountain on the Mediterranean coast of Lebanon to the north of Canaan. It was well-wooded and many vines and flowers grew there so that the fragrance of Lebanon was proverbial (Song of Songs 4:11). If the glory of nature shrivels up

before the LORD, how much more the pride of man? Bashan and
Carmel were not the sort of places liable to be affected by drought,
but the LORD can reverse their condition. If that is so, who then can
resist him? Who is not vulnerable?

The mountains quake before him and the hills melt away
(*verse 5*) intensifies the argument. The LORD is the one who causes
earthquakes and volcanic eruptions (Psalm 97:5; see on Micah
1:4). What seemed most stable – the mountains – quake at him (Isa.
64:1). The LORD is in control of nature, and the forces of nature
cause terror and devastation among the inhabitants of the world.
**The earth trembles at his presence, the world and all who live
in it**. Compare Isaiah 2:19,21.

The conclusion is drawn by means of two rhetorical questions.
**Who can withstand his indignation? Who can endure his fierce
anger?** (*verse 6*). The answer is clearly implied that this is not
possible for anyone (Psalms 76:7; 130:3; Mal. 3:2). **His wrath is
poured out like fire; the rocks are shattered before him**. That is
the reality that all those who are his adversaries, who are opposed
to him, have to reckon with.

Scripture consistently asserts the reality of divine judgment on
sin. The gospel message is twofold: there is the proclamation of the
acceptability before God that is achieved through faith in him and
his provision in Christ; and there is also the proclamation that his
wrath 'is being revealed from heaven against all the ungodlessness
and wickedness of men' (Rom. 1:17,18). To minimise the reality
of God's righteous wrath against sin is to debase his holiness, to
demean the significance of the cross, and to leave in frightful peril
those who do not recognise the enormity of their conduct in the
sight of God. Nahum's message here is an essential part of the
statement of the whole revelation God has made of himself.

It is also the case that it is from the confession of God as creator
and sustainer of the universe that Nahum argues to the impending
judgment against the nations that make light of his requirements.
Nations are without excuse because the eternal power and divine
nature of God has been made plain to them (Rom. 1:18-20).

Nahum 1:7-11: The Kindness and Sternness of the LORD

There is no stepping back from the reality of God's retributive justice, but Nahum now views it against a broader background. When the LORD vindicates his name, it is a two-sided operation. He pours out his furious wrath on those who have set themselves against him, but he also extends his protection and favour to those who are in covenant relationship with him (1:7,8). Nahum then proceeds to focus on how this sternness works itself out in the doom that awaits Assyria (1:9-11).

The kindness of God (1:7). Nahum frequently turns swiftly from one subject to another. No sooner has he ended 1:6 with 'His wrath is poured out like fire; the rocks are shattered before him' than he proceeds **The LORD is good** (*verse 7*). The jarring effect of the change emphasises the contrast that is being made. God's wrath is one aspect of his character that is almost too awesome to contemplate. Its implications for sinners are so overwhelming that we shrink from it. But there is another attribute of God that his people have to remember so as to have a full orbed appreciation of the God with whom they have to do.

Now 'goodness' may be ascribed to the LORD in various ways. For example, it may denote God as implacably opposed to what is morally wrong, and as himself the standard by which all goodness is determined. As such he stands apart from, and over against, his fallen creation, of whom 'there is no one righteous, not even one... there is no one who does good, not even one' (Rom. 3:10,12). It is this aspect of the LORD's goodness that we find in Psalm 25:8 where he is described as 'good and upright', and therefore the one who is supremely qualified to teach sinners the way.

God is also good in the sense that he is the source and provider of good things for all his creation. 'The LORD is good to all', as David reminds us (Psalm 145:9). But the benefit the LORD provides is supremely to be found in the realm of salvation. This provides the basis of the exhortation, 'Give thanks to the LORD, for he is good. His love endures for ever' (Psalm 136:1). This is his covenant love towards those he has chosen to be his people. It is seen not only in the forgiveness he extends (Psalm 86:5), but also in all his subsequent acts of covenant blessing towards those whose hope is in him and who seek him (Lam. 3:25).

This goodness is particularly encountered when his people find themselves in adverse circumstances of the most severe sort in life. He is **a refuge in times of trouble**. This is a general description, and is not confined to any one time in history. It applies whenever a person feels he is up against it – whatever 'it' may be. The word 'trouble' covers both intense turmoil in external circumstances, and inner distress. Then the LORD acts as a 'refuge' (Psalms 18:2; 62:7,8; 91:2), an impregnable mountain fortress which, since it cannot be taken by the enemy, provides security for the one who has felt himself about to go down in battle. 'God is faithful; he will not let you be tempted beyond what you can bear. But when you are tempted, he will also provide a way out so that you can stand up under it' (1 Cor. 10:13).

What is the basis for all this? **He cares for those who trust in him**. Literally, it is he 'knows' them, but it is not just with that knowledge which God has of everything, because he is omniscient. It refers to that covenant knowledge which said of Abraham, 'I know him' (Gen. 18:19, cf. AV); that knowledge which said of Israel 'You only have I known of all the families of the earth' (Amos 3:2, cf. AV); that knowledge of which the Good Shepherd speaks when he says 'I know my sheep' (John 10:14). It is the King of the covenant bestowing recognition upon those who are his. He has chosen them, and so is committed to providing for their needs (Psalm 23:1,2).

The recipients of this protection are 'those who trust in him'. The underlying picture is still that of the fortress. The LORD's people are described as those who 'take refuge' in him (Psalm 62:5-8). This is the recourse of the faithful when they are aware of their own frailty, and so commit their security to God (Psalm 61:2,3). It is not a one-off response that is described, but an ever-recurring characteristic of his people who have as their motto, 'God is our refuge and strength, an ever-present help in trouble' (Psalm 46:1).

The Sternness of God (1:8). But there are two sides to the LORD's action, as Paul brings out. 'Consider therefore the kindness and sternness of God: sternness to those who fell, but kindness to you, provided that you continue in his kindness' (Rom. 11:22). Nahum too recognises this as he says, **but with an overwhelming flood he will make an end of [Nineveh]** (*verse 8*).

Describing judgment in terms of a flood goes back to the days of Noah. Sometimes it conveys the idea of an invading army sweeping through a country (Isa. 8:7,8), and that may be what is foretold here. Though Nineveh is not named, it is clearly indicated (and hence the NIV supplement in brackets). When Nineveh fell, it was as a result of enemy invasion. But there is also the possibility that Nahum's reference here is to an actual flood. Later in 2:6 he distinctly mentions the flooding of the city as contributing to its capture.

He will pursue his foes into darkness. The LORD is himself light (Psalm 27:1; Isa. 10:17), and so brings light to those who enjoy the favour of his presence (Psalms 4:6; 36:9; 97:11). Darkness indicates the condition of those from whom his favour is withdrawn (Micah 7:8). It is the darkness of defeat, and of terror, where God is not. As Job put it, 'There are those who rebel against the light, who do not know its ways or stay in its paths' (Job 24:13). Ultimately, it signifies the eternal doom of godless men 'for whom blackest darkness has been reserved for ever' (Jude 13).

Evil Plots Frustrated (1:9-11). This section poses a number of problems for translators, as can be seen by the variations in the different versions. The NIV translation represents a widely accepted way of understanding the passage, and we shall keep to it in the following comments.

Whatever they plot against the LORD he will bring to an end (*verse 9*). This continues the theme of what happens to the LORD's foes. They had not stumbled into sin against the LORD, but had deliberately embarked on such a policy. All their scheming will, however, be of no avail, for 'there is no wisdom, no insight, no plan, that can succeed against the LORD' (Prov. 21:30). In words recalling the end awaiting Nineveh (1:8), the LORD's action on behalf of his people 'will bring to an end' all their intrigues (Compare Psalm 2). Indeed, it goes a bit further than a promise of what will happen in the future. It is implied that the LORD is already acting to bring their schemes to an end for he is the one who 'foils the plans of the nations' (Psalm 33:10).

Trouble will not come a second time. That looks back to 'the times of trouble' mentioned in 1:7. When Nineveh is struck down by the LORD, no more trouble shall arise from that source to vex the people of God.

Nahum continues 'For', although this is not found at the beginning of 1:10 in the NIV, because he wants to give the reason why there will be no more trouble from Nineveh. Three terse descriptions that are difficult to translate are presented.

(1) **They will be entangled among thorns** (*verse 10*). The thorns are the prickly and useless bushes of the parched wilderness. Nothing much else could be done with them, but to burn them where they lie (2 Sam. 23:7). To become entangled with them was to be presented with an immediate problem that prevented attention being given to anything else. The Assyrians are going to be beset with many troubles. They will have so much on their hands that they will not have time to vex other peoples. That is one reason why there will be no more trouble from that source.

(2) They will be **drunk from their wine**. Two thoughts seem to lie behind this picture. The first is the ease and false sense of security that will characterise the foes of the LORD even when disaster is already threatening them. Zephaniah described Nineveh as the 'carefree city' (Zeph. 2:15). There is also the idea of their helplessness when they are engulfed by their fate (Isaiah 19:14; 24:20). They have become so stupefied by alcohol that they cannot take action to defend themselves (see on 3:11).

(3) **They will be consumed like dry stubble**. The sun soon dried out the stalks left in the ground after harvesting, and they were readily combustible. The burning of stubble is found throughout

the Old Testament (Exod. 15:7; Mal. 4:1) as an illustration of the LORD's judgment sweeping out of existence those who are the objects of his wrath. Here the completeness of their downfall is underlined in that they are likened to 'dry' stubble. There will be no difficulty in setting light to it, and once it is ablaze, there will be no putting it out.

In **From you, [O Nineveh,]** (*verse 11*) the form of 'you' in the Hebrew warrants the identification of the one addressed as Nineveh, which the NIV has made clear. **Has one come forth** refers to a specific individual, probably Sennacherib, who was the most powerful Assyrian aggressor against Judah. The *Annals of Sennacherib* relate how he captured Lachish and 47 fortified cities of Judah. He claimed he had carried away 200,150 people besides multitudes of animals. He also exacted heavy tribute from Hezekiah, and had planned to deport the people (2 Kings 18:14-16,32).

Sennacherib is instanced as an outstanding example of the behaviour described in 1:9. He **plots evil against the LORD**. His emissary to Jerusalem disparaged trust in the LORD (2 Kings 18:30,35). The Assyrian monarch had insulted and blasphemed against the LORD, heaping insults on him (2 Kings 19:22,23). He **counsels wickedness**. 'Wickedness' is 'belial', a term which indicated 'worthlessness, something done without moral principle.' In the inter-testamental period it came to be used as an epithet for Satan. Such a usage is not established as early as Nahum's time, but it does indicate the background against which we are to view the policy of the Assyrian kings. Their conduct was unprincipled and directly antagonistic to the LORD and his people.

Nahum 1:12-2:2: On the Right Hand and on the Left

Nahum continues to develop the theme of 1:7,8, that the LORD's intervention to vindicate his name has two quite different results. The destinies of Nineveh and Judah are juxtaposed throughout this section, with abrupt, unsignalled changes of subject: Judah (1:12,13); Nineveh (1:14); Judah (1:15); Nineveh (2:1); Judah (2:2). The NIV softens the jarring effect of the original by introducing (in underbrackets) Judah in 1:12, and Nineveh in 1:14 and 2:1. But the succession of abrupt moves is a deliberate feature of Nahum's style. It evokes the disturbed and disjointed nature of the times when Nineveh would fall. More significantly, it brings into effective contrast the twofold destinies of the parties he is talking about. This is a theme that is found throughout Scripture – the parting of the ways that the LORD effects in his judgment, especially at the last day. 'He will put the sheep on his right and the goats on his left' (Matt. 25:33).

Judah (1:12,13). In 1:12 Nahum for the first time presents the direct speech of the LORD. He introduces it with the words, **This is what the LORD says** (*verse 12*). Although this phrase occurs only here in his book, it is frequently used by other prophets to indicate that they were acting as the LORD's messengers, passing on what he had said to them (Micah 2:3; 3:5).

The LORD presents himself as the liberator of his people. His intervention means the downfall of their enemies. **Although they have allies and are numerous** indicates that it does not matter what the power of the enemy is, or how many supporters they can call on to provide them with reinforcements. Their strength will prove inadequate when the LORD moves against them. **They will be cut off** uses a word that elsewhere refers to the shearing of sheep (Gen. 38:12) or the mowing of a meadow (Psalm 72:6). It is a close cropping that awaits Nineveh, which will also **pass away**. Often when cities were captured, they were not totally destroyed, and many of their inhabitants would remain in them as subjects of the conqueror. Here there is the first intimation that Nineveh's fate is going to be different: not just capture, but annihilation. After it was taken, it quickly fell into decay, and the site was forgotten until 19th century archaeologists uncovered it.

Then the LORD brings out the significance of his action for Judah. **Although I have afflicted you** indicates that there is no denying that the LORD's fatherly chastisement of them because of their wilful disobedience had resulted in their being brought low in suffering and pain. 'No discipline seems pleasant at the time, but painful' (Heb. 12:11). The Assyrian armies had been the LORD's instrument to bring his erring people to their senses. But now the time to show favour has come (Psalm 102:13), and so he promises **I will afflict you no more**, that is, on account of their past sins.

Now (*verse 13*) emphasises that though the promised change is still future, it will not be long in coming. **I will break their yoke from your neck and tear your shackles away**. A yoke was a shaped piece of wood placed across the necks of two oxen, enabling them to work together in pulling a plough or cart. It was also used, as here, to refer to the rigours of political subjugation by a foreign power (Deut. 28:48; Isa. 47:6). Breaking off such a yoke gave freedom to those who were oppressed (Isa. 14:25). Similarly the shackles, probably of metal, that restrained their movement so that as prisoners and slaves they could not escape, would be done away with.

Nineveh (1:14). Nahum then switches his focus. Nineveh is addressed, or it may on this occasion be the king of Nineveh, representing the people, and the divine decree is announced. **The LORD has given a command concerning you, [Nineveh]** (*verse 14*). The matter is fixed (Isa. 14:24-27). The order has gone out to those who are to be the instruments for effecting the LORD's purpose. **You will have no descendants to bear your name**. This takes up the prediction of 1:12 that 'they will be cut off and pass away'. The defeat that is coming on them is of the most sweeping sort, involving national extermination. They will have no offspring to perpetuate their national identity (Psalm 109:13).

I will destroy the carved images and cast idols that are in the temple of your gods. The Assyrians worshipped many gods, Ishtar and Nabu in particular having outstanding shrines erected to them in Nineveh. Whenever the Assyrians captured another land, it was their custom to show the power of their own gods by pillaging the temples of those they had conquered, and bringing the booty to adorn the temples of Nineveh. Now it is their own temples that are to be desecrated. Their gods, of whom they had so many, would be shown to be powerless, just as God had exposed the worthlessness of the deities worshipped in Egypt (Exod. 12:12).

There is no future for Assyria. **I will prepare your grave**. This is a prophecy of national extinction. **For you are vile**, of little significance, no matter what they thought of themselves. Their deep rooted iniquity has led the Almighty to despise them, and regard them with utter contempt. 'Those who honour me I will honour, but those who despise me will be disdained' (1 Sam. 2:30).

Judah (1:15). Then Nahum cites words from Isaiah 52:7 to describe the joyful arrival in Judah of a messenger who proclaims deliverance. **Look, there on the mountains, the feet of one who brings good news, who proclaims peace!** *(verse 15)*. The herald is seen as coming over the mountains from a distant land. He is telling of the overthrow of their oppressor: Nineveh is defeated. The people may now enjoy restoration to all the privileges of dwelling in the land in tranquillity and with divine blessing.

These words had earlier been used by Isaiah when he looked forward to Israel's deliverance from Babylon. Paul later uses them of the spread of the gospel message throughout the nations (Rom. 10:15). This is an instance of where the prophets are led to see the general vista of the divine deliverance from the captivity imposed by the enemies of the LORD's people on them, and are more aware of the similarities in God's way of working than of the precise time scale on which it is worked out. See on Micah 4:1.

The response to this good news is to be expressed in worship, because it is God who has been their deliverer and who should be thanked (Psalm 107:8). **Celebrate your festivals, O Judah**. The removal of the influence of foreign pagan rulers would permit the worship of Judah to be reinstated in purity, while the religion of Assyria was destroyed (1:14). **Fulfil your vows** refers no doubt to the many prayers made for deliverance with solemn promises to honour the LORD when he answered prayer. Therefore when the LORD's goodness has been experienced, it is time to show that these pledges were not empty gestures (Psalm 116:14,18).

No more will the wicked invade you resumes the theme of the end of 1:9. The word for 'the wicked' is Belial, which is also found in 1:11 where it is translated 'wickedness'. Here Nineveh is being viewed as an embodiment of the hostile power of evil. **They will be completely destroyed.** In her ruination there is a foreshadowing of what will happen to all the malignant powers of evil assembled against the people of God.

Nineveh (2:1). Then Nahum goes back to telling what the future holds in store for Nineveh, as he graphically portrays the vision he has had of its overthrow. **An attacker advances against you, [Nineveh]** (*verse 1*). The word 'attacker' presents the enemy as intent on smashing Nineveh to pieces and scattering them on all sides (Psalm 68:1; Isa. 24:1). Nahum hears a series of abrupt military commands being given, as the Assyrians get ready to resist the invasion. **Guard the fortress, watch the road, brace yourselves, marshal all your strength!** But all their military watchfulness will be to no avail, as Nahum will spell out in detail throughout the rest of his prophecy.

Judah (2:2). But before that, there is one further switch back to the LORD's people. The closer the hostile forces get to Nineveh, the nearer is the restitution of their fortunes. **The LORD will restore the splendour of Jacob, like the splendour of Israel** (*verse 2*). Jacob here refers to Judah, the southern kingdom, but the comparison with Israel is not so clear. It may be to the glories of the united kingdom back in the days of David and Solomon. Alternatively, this may pick up a theme that was common in the prophets (Micah 5:3), as they looked forward to the time when the divided and scattered people of God would be found united once more, even **though destroyers have laid them waste and have ruined their vines.** Vines played an important role in the agriculture of Palestine, and indeed the vine was a symbol for Israel (Psalm 80:8-16). Despite the devastation they have suffered, the LORD is able to remedy their situation.

Nahum delivered this message to the people of God at a time when they were dejected and suffering from the ravages and oppression of the adversary. It was not intended to provide a warning to Nineveh, for the Assyrians no longer had ears to hear such a message. But those they oppressed were provided with hope through the message of divinely provided deliverance. There is a gleam here of the victory that the Messiah would bring to his people. Just as Nahum cites Isaiah 52:7 in 1:15a, so too would Paul in Romans 10:15, applying the words to the preaching of the gospel. The immediate deliverance of God's people, whether from Nineveh or Babylon, was but part of the total divine pledge of redemption from all thralldom by evil. This pledge is ultimately fulfilled in the deliverance that is effected by Christ (Hebrews 2:15).

Nahum 2:3-13: "I Am Against You"

Nahum resumes his prophecy of the downfall of Nineveh, the capital of the Assyrian empire, from 2:1, where notice had been given of the approaching forces. Now they have arrived at the capital, and are vividly described (2:3,4). 2:5,6 tells of the fall of the city, and the next section, 2:7-10, deals with the aftermath of its collapse. In 2:11,12 there is an extended comparison made between Nineveh and a lion, which leads into the significant, interpretative pronouncement, " 'I am against you,' declares the LORD Almighty" (2:13). It is his opposition to the city that is being outworked in her capture by enemy forces.

The downfall of the Assyrian Empire began in the closing years of Ashurbanipal's reign (669-626 B.C.). The details are obscure because the Assyrian records for the period have not survived, but by 626 Babylon had successfully asserted its independence under Nabopolassar. Events proved too much for Sin-shar-ishkun (623-612 B.C.) as other tributary states, including Judah, repudiated his control. Various forces pressed into Assyrian territory capturing major centres, including the former capital Asshur, which fell to the Medes in 614 B.C. In 612 the Medes, along with the Babylonians, and apparently also the Scythians – a nomadic people from Central Asia who were making their presence felt in Mesopotamia at this time, and who had at first helped the Assyrians – surrounded Nineveh. Sieges of cities well-fortified against attack could be protracted, but Nineveh fell in August 612 B.C. after only three months.

The vivid description enables us to envisage the scene around Nineveh during this siege, because Nahum's prophecy was fulfilled in detail. **The shields of his soldiers are red; the warriors are clad in scarlet** (*verse 3*). 'His' refers back to the 'attacker' of 2:1. The shields would have had a wooden frame with leather stretched over it, and were probably coloured red, rather than being red because of blood stains. 'Scarlet' seems to refer to the colour of the uniforms they wore. The appearance of the troops outside the city wall was impressive and designed to be intimidating.

Further details are given of the besieging army. **The metal on the chariots flashes on the day they are made ready**. Chariots were the most advanced weaponry of the time, and were particularly used for fighting in open country. They had a light wooden frame, with wood, leather, and metal fitments, which would flash in the sun. A chariot had one axle for ease of movement, and was pulled by two horses. It could have as many as four men in it: a driver, an archer, and two shield bearers to protect them. **The spears of pine are brandished**, as the waiting troops are drilled, and practise the manoeuvres they will employ.

In the next verse Nahum continues his description of the activity of the chariots. **The chariots storm through the streets, rushing back and forth through the squares** (*verse 4*). Mention of 'streets' and 'squares' presents an interesting problem: is this before or after the fall of the city?

Nineveh was built on the east bank of the river Tigris and seems to have been surrounded by two defensive structures. One was an inner defensive wall between 11 and 13 kilometres (7-8 miles) in circumference and about 18-30 metres (60-100 feet) in height. This wall was so thick that three chariots could pass on its top. It had defence towers 60 metres (200 feet) tall and 15 gates by which entry could be made into the city. Outside it there was a moat 45 metres (150 feet) wide, filled with water diverted from two of the smaller rivers which flowed through the city. Apart from the western side of the city where the river Tigris provided a barrier, there was a further defensive structure which lay further out again. It consisted of a series of earthworks – ramparts and ditches – to prevent an enemy from coming close. Between the inner wall and the outer defences would be found the suburbs of the city, and it seems to be in this area that Nahum sees the chariots storming through the streets.

This would also fit in with what we know of the course of the siege of Nineveh. There seem to have been three decisive periods of fighting. The first, near the beginning, was won by the Assyrians, and left the enemy forces outside the outer defences. There are records which suggest that this victory led to a bout of drinking celebrations within the city. When this was reported by a deserter to the Medo-Babylonian forces, they suddenly attacked, and entered the area up to the inner wall. It is at this stage of the attack that 2:4 fits. The third stage of the fall of the city was when the inner defences were penetrated (2:6).

Nahum envisages the demoralising impact of seeing the chariots move impressively through the city suburbs before the final fall of the city. **They look like flaming torches; they dart about like lightning**.

Nahum then moves on to describe the final stage of the siege. **He summons his picked troops, yet they stumble on their way** (*verse 5*). At first this might suggests that 'he' is the Assyrian king, and even his finest men are unable to fight properly, and can only lurch into battle somewhat uncertainly. However, the verse continues, **They dash to the city wall; the protective shield is put in place**. 'The protective shield' was a covering used by those besieging a city to screen themselves from missiles hurled down at them as they approached the city walls. The troops at the end of the verse are definitely those attacking Nineveh, and the whole verse probably refers to them. The attacking commander summons his crack troops to try to breach the inner wall. They rush up to it. Is it the ease of their advance that causes them to stumble as they hurry forward at an unexpectedly quick pace? Or, is it that they stumble over the rubble that has come from ruined buildings near the wall? They move swiftly forwards and protect themselves as they begin to use battering rams to breach the inner walls.

We would then have expected a record of the success of their manoeuvre. Instead another aspect of the situation is introduced. It takes five words in the original to tell starkly of the overthrow of Nineveh. **The river gates are thrown open and the palace collapses** (*verse 6*). 'Collapses' is literally 'is dissolved', and pictures the mud bricks, of which almost all structures in Mesopotamia were built, washed away by the force of water.

Nineveh had fifteen gates in its inner wall, and all were near or on one of the rivers of the city, but it does not seem as if 2:6 tells about these. The unusual phrase 'the gates of the rivers' seems rather to refer to dams and sluices that were used to control the flow of the two tributaries of the Tigris that actually went through the city, and which had caused flooding in the past. Perhaps the water supply had at first been cut off, and then in the month Ab (July/ August) when the rivers attain their greatest height, the enemy opened the 'river gates'. At any rate the river is recorded by a later Greek historian to have breached the city walls and flattened them to let the invading armies in. Archaeologists have found flood debris at the highest ancient level of settlement in Nineveh. With the ensuing destruction of the palace, all resistance collapses and the city is taken.

The first word of 2:7 has caused considerable perplexity, but the NIV rendering is as good as any: **It is decreed that [the city] be exiled and carried away** (*verse 7*). Just as the Assyrians had done to many others, so it would happen to their own capital. **Its slave girls moan like doves and beat upon their breasts**. This is a picture of distress and wailing over the catastrophe that has engulfed them.

Now after the city is taken, Nahum actually names Nineveh.

Nineveh is like a pool, and its water is draining away (*verse 8*). 'Pool' refers to part of an irrigation system (2 Kings 20:20; Eccles. 2:6). When its wall is holed, it can no longer contain water. Opinions differ as to whether the water flowing out of the pool represents the riches of Nineveh, or its population, leaving the city. The NIV translation seems to favour the latter. We hear officials shouting out to the fleeing people (and troops). **"Stop! Stop!" they cry, but no one turns back**. The city has been so devastated that they only think to escape from it. Perhaps this represented a reaction to an old superstition that the city would only fall when the river became its enemy, as was now the case.

We then hear another set of cries in the confusion of the fallen city. It is the voice of the invader shouting, **Plunder the silver! Plunder the gold! The supply is endless, the wealth from all its treasures!** (*verse 9*). Assyria had looted the lands it had defeated. Those who became tributary states were forced to pay heavy taxes, as Israel and Judah had often found out to their cost (2 Kings 17:3,4; 18:14-16). The wealth had flowed back to Assyria, and particularly to the capital, which became the richest city in the east. Now it has fallen, and is being subjected to the same treatment it had shown to others.

She is pillaged, plundered, stripped! (*verse 10*) renders a very effective play by Nahum on three similarly sounding words to reinforce the totality of the devastation of the city. Such features generally defy effective translation. 'Desolate, desolated, desolation' is a very poor attempt to convey the way he builds up this picture of ruin.

The inhabitants of the city are shattered and demoralised by what has happen to them. **Hearts melt, knees give way, bodies tremble, every face grows pale** lists the outward symptoms of their inward devastation. Fear and bewilderment grip all.

The prophet emphasises the helplessness of Nineveh by using a mocking analogy. **Where now is the lions' den, the place where they fed their young, where the lion and lioness went, and the cubs, with nothing to fear?** (*verse 11*). The lion is described in the

Old Testament as 'mighty among beasts, who retreats before nothing' (Prov. 30:30). The violence of wicked men is often likened to the lion's savage attacks (Psalms 10:9; 17:12). The comparison also fitted the Assyrians because their kings compared themselves to lions in their terrible power. Lions featured prominently in the artwork on many Assyrian buildings. Once they had been able to behave like the lions, going about with no opposition. There had been no reason for them to fear, but now the situation has changed. Even their place of security has been destroyed.

The lion killed enough for his cubs and strangled the prey for his mate, filling his lairs with the kill and his dens with the prey (*verse 12*). The emphasis in this verse is on the killing of the prey by which the lion more than adequately provided for its own. In the art of the Ancient East lions are frequently represented strangling their prey. That was how Assyria too had behaved. It was not just a matter of gathering wealth into her capital, but doing so by violence and cruelty (see on 3:1).

This section then draws to a conclusion by looking beyond the human actors on the stage of history to the ultimate and controlling reality, the LORD and his opposition to Assyria's rapine and pillaging. **"I am against you," declares the LORD Almighty** (*verse 13*). There can be no greater threat uttered against the city than the LORD's opposition to it. 'The LORD Almighty' is the NIV rendering corresponding to 'the LORD of hosts' in the AV. It refers to God as the one who is in control of all the powers that are. He who has at his behest whatever forces exist in the universe has declared himself the enemy of Nineveh, and that is why this total destruction is going to ensue. No matter what power man may think he has, no matter what preparations he has gone to great trouble to make – if the LORD of hosts declares himself against him, it is all futile and doomed to collapse.

The two themes of the section, the invading army and the analogy to lions, are brought together in this verse. **I will burn up your chariots in smoke, and the sword will devour your young lions**. It is the LORD himself who is active in the affairs of man. A true understanding of history requires that we look beyond second causes to God himself, who causes their finest weaponry to be burned. The 'young lions' is a poetic designation for Nineveh's soldiers. **I will leave you no prey on the earth** continues the picture of 2:12. It implies no prey is left because the predator himself has been removed.

The voices of your messengers will no longer be heard. At one level this spells out the end of the empire. The heralds would have carried the royal proclamations to the most distant parts of the realm. Nineveh's commands would have been made known, and also the demands for tribute. But that is now all over. The rule of Assyria is broken.

There is also an implicit contrast with 1:15, where the messengers of Judah had brought her good news. This reminds us once more of the contrasting destinies of the people of God and of their adversaries.

Nineveh was a rich, powerful, and magnificent city, which arrogantly said, 'I am, and there is none besides me' (Zeph. 2:15). But her prosperity was not founded on righteousness. Therefore the LORD of hosts declares, 'I am against you', and divine justice makes it inevitable that disaster will come on those who have such a sentence pronounced against them. The sack of Nineveh represents the defeat of evil, as the LORD punishes Assyria, renowned for its cruelty, for the atrocities it had perpetrated.

Nahum 3:1-7: The City of Blood

The third chapter of Nahum is a brilliant piece of poetry, which again tells of the overthrow of Nineveh. But it does not just go over ground that has already been covered. Each of the three sections of the chapter emphasises one particular lesson that has to be learned from the situation. The first section (3:1-7) shows that the city has brought her downfall on herself by her sin and her crimes against humanity. The God who controls all things has not set himself capriciously against Nineveh. In 3:5 he repeats his earlier declaration, 'I am against you.' God's sovereign rule over all nations is righteous. His retribution matches what comes on Nineveh to what she has done. 'Do not be deceived: God cannot be mocked. A man reaps what he sows' (Gal. 6:7).

Many features recorded in chapter 3 are also found in Babylonian and Greek sources recording the sack of Nineveh. There are those who deny the existence of truly predictive prophecy and account for these facts by supposing that Nahum was written up after the event as a hymn of praise to God for the overthrow of the capital of the evil empire. That, however, is to dismiss as fabricated the evident standpoint of the book, that Judah was still oppressed (1:9,12,13), and Nineveh's downfall awaited. Instead, these parallels are to be understood as evidence that the prophet did not speak from merely human knowledge, but was divinely inspired. Furthermore, when news about Nineveh did reach Judah, the many correspondences between the events in the news and the words of the prophet would have strengthened the faith of those who waited on the LORD for his deliverance.

There are five charges raised against Nineveh in this section: brutality, deceit, and pillaging in 3:1, and harlotry and sorcery in 3:3.

Woe! (*verse 1*) is normally used to bewail the dead, but is also employed by the prophets to introduce a dire warning, as if the one addressed were already as good as dead (see on Micah 2:1). Nahum here addresses Nineveh as **the city of blood**, literally 'of bloods', the plural being used in Hebrew to signify blood shed by violence. War inevitably involves bloodshed, and can easily lead to atrocities. But the Assyrians gloried in violence, and made the committing of atrocities an instrument of their policy for subduing conquered peoples. With delight and pride the annals of the Assyrian kings describe the tortures that were used. Their wall pictures frequently show their victims with limbs torn off, or eyes gouged out, or treated as animals, or impaled, or flayed -- spread out, pinned face down to the ground, and their skin systematically and completely removed from their living bodies. The Assyrian regime had for centuries deliberately employed such brutality to keep under their terror-stricken subjects.

The indictment continues with **full of lies**. This seems to deal with official statements made to secure the submission of weaker nations. Why fight them, if they will give in to false promises? We have a notable instance of this in the speech of the emissary of the Assyrian king to the besieged inhabitants of Jerusalem. 'This is what the king of Assyria says: Make peace with me and come out to me. Then everyone of you will eat from his own vine and fig tree and drink water from his own cistern, until I come and take you to a land like your own, a land of grain and new wine, a land of bread and vineyards, a land of olive trees and honey. Choose life and not death!' (2 Kings 18:31,32). This indifference towards truth may also be traced in the boasting records left by many of its kings, and ancient accounts of the business trickery of the merchants of the city.

The next item is **full of plunder, never without victims**. 'Victims' looks back to the description of the lions' prey in 2:12. The history of Assyrian imperial expansionism is one long record of pillaging and depredation, justifying the comparison with a ferocious animal snatching whatever it could. Assyria had grown rich at the expense of other nations.

It is not clear how we should understand 3:2,3. Many suggest that Nahum switches suddenly from the charges he is levying against Nineveh to a preview of its destruction. While such a switch would be in keeping with his style, it is just as probable that what we have here is a picture of the way in which the Assyrian forces bore down upon their hapless victims. **The crack of whips, the clatter of wheels, galloping horses and jolting chariots! Charging cavalry, flashing swords, and glittering spears! Many casualties, piles of dead, bodies without number, people stumbling over the corpses** (*verses 2,3*). It is a picture of slaughter and carnage on all sides, and describes both the way the Assyrians had behaved towards others and what they were going to experience themselves.

What had been happening is to be explained in terms of the Assyrians' own behaviour. **All because of the wanton lust of a harlot** (*verse 4*). Frequently 'harlot' is used in the Old Testament to apply to Israel when she was unfaithful to the LORD and deserted him to engage in idol worship (Isa. 1:21; Jer. 3:1-3). The covenant bond was a solemn pledging of one party to the other, as in marriage. So when Israel broke her covenant commitments, she became an adulteress spiritually. What was more, in the debased rituals of pagan shrines she was practically involved in uncleanness (Jer. 2:20).

But this is Assyria. She had never made any covenant commitment to the LORD from which she could fall away. There was no bond between the LORD and Assyria to which she could be unfaithful, apart from the basic bond of all mankind to the Creator. The point of the comparison here seems rather to be to the harlot as one who gives her services out for hire. She was out for personal gain, and **alluring** brings out the devices she was prepared to use to draw others to her. There was the splendour of her wealth and power. What a one to have as an ally!

An instance of Assyrian willingness to sell their services is found in Judean history. When Rezin king of Syria and Pekah the son of Remaliah king of Israel made war against Judah, Ahaz sent messengers to Tiglath-Pileser, who then ruled Assyria, and became his ally and tributary (2 Kings 16:5- 9). But it was to prove a very one-sided bargain.

Nineveh is also described as **the mistress of sorceries**, one who understood and practised black arts. There have been recovered thousands of tablets which show the abysmal superstition that existed. Astrology flourished as a means of foretelling the future. Good luck charms made from many materials were worn to ward off evil spirits, who were thought to exist on every side waiting to plague their victims. Sorcerers would be involved both in trying to foretell the future and in trying to induce these demons to attack particular victims.

By her use of such means Nineveh **enslaved nations by her prostitution and peoples by her witchcraft**, selling her services wherever it would pay off and terrorising others by threats of demonic action. She 'sold' nations and their peoples into slavery.

No action was beneath her if it would advance her purposes and contribute to her gain. Here is the capital city of an empire characterised by ruthless oppression, depravity, and the advancement of her own power.

But **"I am against you," declares the LORD Almighty** (*verse 5*). This re-echoes 2:13. He is opposed to all behaviour which defies his authority and disregards the rights of others. Military might or economic power do not render a nation immune from the scrutiny of the LORD of hosts, to whom all he has created in heaven and earth are answerable. His condemnation of Nineveh means that she will receive a punishment that matches her crime of being a harlot. **I will lift your skirts over your face**. She had been ready to expose her nakedness in the course of her trade, but now it will be exposed to her shame (Jer. 13:26; Ezek. 16:35-39). She had enslaved nations, stripping her captives naked and exposing them to humiliation, but she herself will now be humiliated, as later Babylon would be also (Isa. 47:3). **I will show the nations your nakedness and the kingdoms your shame**. She will become an abject international spectacle to be viewed and derided by all the nations.

I will pelt you with filth (*verse 6*). God continues to effect his judgment through human agents. He will permit those he brings against Nineveh to throw at her any loathsome object on which they can lay hand. The word 'filth' is often used to describe idols and idol worship as 'detestable' in God's sight (2 Chron. 15:8; Ezek. 5:11). Here again Nineveh receives a fitting punishment. **I will treat you with contempt and make you a spectacle**. When Nineveh is exposed and displayed as a spectacle of God's derision, people will know that his verdict on her has been executed.

All who see you will flee from you (*verse 7*). They will look for a moment and then flee away in consternation at what has become of her. As they do so, they will say, **"Nineveh is in ruins – who will mourn for her?"** They express no regret at what has happened to her. They have no sympathy for her, and are sure no one else will be prepared even to pay last respects to her with decent funeral rites. God too recognises that all have been alienated from Nineveh, because the answer to the question he poses, **Where can I find anyone to comfort you?**, implies that there will be no one interested in giving even a word of encouragement to those left in Nineveh's ruins.

Nahum 3:8-11: Learning from History

In the second section of chapter 3 (3:8-11) Nahum compares Nineveh to another great city of the ancient world. By using what happened to it he demonstrates that a similar fate can overtake Nineveh, and so he encourages the people of God to look forward to his intervention against their enemy.

The NIV margin tells us that the Hebrew name of the city Nahum uses as his example was No Amon: No represents the Egyptian word for 'city', and Amon (who was its principal god) the sun god. No Amon is better known to us as Thebes, one of the names the Greeks gave it.

Thebes was in upper (i.e. southern) Egypt, some 480 kilometres (300 miles) south of the modern city of Cairo (see Map I). It was the main city of upper Egypt, and its origins are lost in the mists of antiquity. The city grew to splendour around 2000 B.C., and was the Egyptian capital for long periods. Homer speaks of its wealth, its one hundred gates, and its well-equipped chariots. It had been established on the east bank of the Nile, on a bend where the river sweeps furthest east and enters a broad and fruitful valley. The temples, obelisks, sphinxes, and palaces in the ruins at Karnak and Luxor are what remain there of the glory of greater Thebes.

Thebes spread across to the west bank of the Nile. Clustered along the foot of steep cliffs and slopes of the Nile valley were the great temples of many generations of pharaohs. Further west, penetrating into the cliffs is the Valley of Kings – where royal tombs of the New Kingdom (1500-1100 B.C.) are found. The picture many have of ancient Egypt is based on the impressive remains of this city.

The rhetorical question, **Are you better than Thebes?** (*verse*

8), was not asked to encourage comparison between the architec-
tural heritage and splendour of Thebes and Nineveh. The focus is
rather on the seeming invulnerability of Thebes as a great and well-
defended city. **Situated on the Nile, with water around her**.
Thebes was situated 'on the rivers', on branches of the Nile, which
at that point is somewhat under a kilometre (about ½ mile) wide and
divides into four channels. There was 'water around her' – not a
reference to what happened when the Nile flooded, but to the
channels of the river and to a moat filled with water from the river.

The river was her defence. The AV has here 'whose rampart
was the sea', reflecting the Hebrew, but not allowing, as the NIV
does, for the fact that the Hebrew word 'sea' can be used for any
large body of water, and is here a term for the Nile itself. There is
thus no geographical blunder, because Thebes was, of course,
hundreds of miles upstream. **The waters her wall** probably refers
to the fact that the river served Thebes in place of a rampart (a
smaller, outer wall) before one reached the great city wall. The
main wall of the city rose from the very edge of the Nile.

Thebes was not only situated in a very strong site. She also had
considerable support from elsewhere. **Cush and Egypt were her
boundless strength** (*verse 9*). 'Cush' refers to the territory south
of Aswan, corresponding to the modern states of Sudan and
Ethiopia. It was from there that the rulers of the Twenty-Fifth
Dynasty of Egypt (730-656 B.C.) originated. 'Egypt' may perhaps
be used in the restricted sense of northern Egypt. Thebes could thus
draw on economic and military resources from north and south. It
was 'boundless', says Nahum, deliberately using the same phrase
that is translated 'endless' in 2:9, and so drawing a comparison
between the resources available to the two cities.

Put and Libya were among her allies. Libya was, and is, to the
west of Egypt, on the north African coast. Put has not been certainly
identified. Many take it as a term for a region in much the same area
as Libya, while others, supposing that Nahum is trying to say that
Thebes could draw on resources from all points of the compass,
argue that Put was a region on the Red Sea coast.

Yet she was taken captive and went into exile (*verse 10*). Despite the advantages conferred on her by her situation and by the allies she could call on to help her, Thebes fell. 'Are you better than her?' This question was rhetorically addressed to Nineveh at the beginning of 3:8. But the challenge is really to the people of God whom Nahum is addressing. They should not doubt his word. Nineveh appeared impregnable. The evil empire was at the height of its power. Nahum's prophecy seemed, if not impossible, then at any rate for the distant future. But he is teaching a lesson from history, and recent history at that. They all knew how disaster had suddenly engulfed Thebes. 'A week in politics is a long time.' Situations that seem impregnable can be turned round in a moment. Powers that seem entrenched for years to come can be overthrown very quickly, as even in recent times we have seen the Soviet Union disintegrate.

The sack of Thebes teaches another lesson. Early critics frequently maintained this was biblical fiction. The records for the period did not allow time for this to happen, and so they maintained Nahum had invented this disaster. But their conclusions were premature, and here, as in many other matters, the discoveries of the archaeologist have vindicated the truthfulness of the biblical narrative. We now have records for this troubled period in Egyptian history. Under the Ethiopian Twenty-Fifth Dynasty, Egypt constantly tried to stir up trouble for Assyria by inciting the smaller states of Palestine to revolt. In two separate campaigns Assyria decisively defeated Egypt. In the first Thebes surrendered (670 B.C.), but in the second (663) it was pillaged and razed.

The Assyrians carried out the task with their customary brutality. **Her infants were dashed to pieces at the head of every street**. They would not have survived the long march to slavery in Assyria, so they were exterminated on the spot. The common people were deported in groups, but **lots were cast for her nobles, and all her great men were put in chains**. Being better educated, they would have been more valuable slaves, and so were allocated to individual captors by lot.

The same fate awaits Nineveh. Thebes had all these great advantages, and what did they benefit her? Nineveh too enjoyed a similar situation and could call on the resources of a vast empire, but no matter how well Nineveh is defended, the same can, and will, happen to her. There is also the further note of the exact retribution that will befall Nineveh, for it was after all the Assyrians who had brought about the downfall of Thebes in so terrible a way. As they had done to others, so it would come upon them.

You too will become drunk (*verse 11*). The picture is of someone who has lost control of his faculties, and is unable to act with calm and deliberation (1:10). Thebes had reeled under the impact of the calamity that engulfed her, so too will Nineveh. **You will go into hiding and seek refuge from the enemy**. There was indeed a remarkable parallel between the Ethiopian Pharaoh, Tanut-amon, who was so unnerved by the approaching Assyrian forces that he abandoned Thebes to seek security further south in the Nile valley. When Nineveh itself fell, the ruling king died in the blaze, but his successor fled to Haran and held out there for a few years before that city too fell before the Babylonians.

Nahum was primarily speaking to the people of Judah in his own day and telling them that an impregnable city can be breached. Every age has to learn that it is easy to be deceived by current appearances. We put our trust in national prosperity and imagine our world and cities are different from those of old. They are not. They are part of the same world, ruled by the same God, who judges by the same standards. He does not condone sin. If we as a generation and civilization do not repent and conform to what God requires of us, it is the same destiny that awaits us also.

Thebes was powerful like Nineveh – and yet Thebes had not oppressed the people of God. Thebes typifies those who live for this life, abounding in wealth, ease and power, forgetful of God. Nineveh is more the image of the world oppressing God's people. If Thebes which did not actively oppose God's cause fell, what shall the end be for those who openly resist him?

Nahum 3:12-19: The Final Collapse

In these concluding verses of his prophecy Nahum, as the LORD's spokesman, focuses on the internal weakness of Nineveh, and how it will contribute to her downfall. He uses a number of themes to make clear what is going to happen to her. She is the 'consumed', the 'eaten', city. The one word in Hebrew underlies 'the eater' of 3:12, 'has consumed' at the end of 3:13, and 'devour' and 'consume' (3:15). He also uses the illustration of a plague of locusts in four different ways (3:15-17). His message is not just that Nineveh will be overthrown by outside forces, but that the strong, cruel, harsh might of imperial Assyria is going to be the victim of its own internal depravity. Neither military might nor economic dominance will be able to avert the catastrophe.

As the enemy encircles them, the people of Nineveh will become demoralised. Not only will they be very frightened, but they will also have lost the moral fibre that is needed to halt corruption sapping their strength and will to resist.

Collapse of Military Might (3:12-15). **All your fortresses are like fig trees with their first ripe fruit** (*verse 12*). Nahum sees the situation that will prevail. Her military strongholds are going to collapse before the enemy. There would be no heroic resistance. The enemy would not need to invent some new weapon to overcome the Assyrians, or devise some tactical masterstroke. It will be like walking up to a fig tree with first ripe fruit and giving it a little shake. Down it comes, but not on to the ground. No, there is the turn given by Nahum to his description. **When they are shaken, the figs fall into the mouth of the eater**. It is a picture of easy success.

Nahum explains why there will be no resistance. **Look at your troops - they are all women!** (*verse 13*). Now that description is used in Scripture to denote weakness, or even cowardice (Isa. 19:16; Jer. 50:37; 51:30). But what Nahum is indicating here is probably something more than that: degeneracy, and effeminacy. That is how Greek history portrays Sin-shar-ishkun, the last king of Nineveh: a frightened, debased pervert. It seems that it was not mere cowardice that led to Nineveh's fall, but cowardice that sprang from moral corruption which had undermined the once strong and cruel race. The NIV does not translate a word that may be rendered 'in the middle of you'. It emphasises that this decay was very much a phenomenon of the capital, Nineveh, and affected those who were in positions of power there.

The gates of your land may refer either to the mountain passes at the borders of the Assyrian heartland, or to strategic fortifications on the route to the city. The troops have not defended them, and so they **are wide open to your enemies**. They have been taken and burned. **Fire has consumed their bars**. The bars were those placed behind the gates to keep them closed. They have been destroyed in the conflagration, and so the fortresses can no longer provide any defence.

In this situation where the way to Nineveh lies wide open, five taunting commands are addressed to the city. **Draw water for the siege!** (*verse 14*). The water supply within Nineveh was insufficient for the city. Most had to be brought in, and such external supplies would be the first thing an advancing army would cut off. Preparations would have to be made to withstand a siege by storing up vast quantities of water.

Strengthen your defences! Work the clay, tread the mortar, repair the brickwork! Stone was a scarce commodity in Mesopotamia, and most construction, including city walls, was made of clay bricks dried in the sun. The vast fortifications of Nineveh would have required huge quantities of bricks for the on-going maintenance of the city walls, quite apart from any additional defences that might have been hastily erected in view of the impending threat.

There (*verse 15*), in the very place where they had expended so much effort and resources, the inadequacy of all they can do will be harshly exposed. **The fire will devour you; the sword will cut you down**. Nahum sees the city ablaze and the people slaughtered by their enemies. Babylonian and Greek records confirm that Nineveh was set on fire.

The rest of 3:15 is rather difficult to understand. The NIV takes it to mean **the sword will cut you down and, like grasshoppers, consume you**. Grasshoppers are not renowned for their propensity to devour, nor would the sword be an effective weapon to use against them. Elsewhere (for example, Jer. 51:14,27) the NIV translates the same word as 'locusts', and that also seems to fit in better with what is required here. Hebrew has a varied selection of words for the locust, and this particular one seems to refer to it at an immature stage when it has no wings and moves about by jumping. The slaughter the enemy forces will inflict on the city will cause as much damage as locusts do when they sweep through a land.

Multiply like grasshoppers, multiply like locusts! 'Grasshoppers' is the same word as before and should be taken as 'locusts', while the word translated as 'locusts' refers to them as swarming insects which come in incredible numbers. If these words continued the earlier imagery of locusts as a source of damage, it is the enemy forces approaching Nineveh that would be bidden to come with a massive military presence and inflict as much damage as possible. Nahum, however, does not otherwise address those who besieged the city, and so it might be preferable to view a change in the use of the locust imagery in the middle of 3:15. Such a change is rendered more probable by the fact that other analogies using locusts are found in the following verses. These words are then spoken to Nineveh, as are those immediately before and after them. They continue the mocking commands to prepare for the onslaught, and the reference to locusts is just to their numbers. Nineveh is to gather as many troops as she possibly could, so that they resemble the locust swarms. But even so, the coming disaster will not be averted.

Collapse of Economic Power (3:16). **You have increased the number of your merchants till they are more than the stars of the sky** (*verse 16*) shows that trade followed Assyria's imperial conquests. Her traders were numerous. The number of the stars is often used to describe the size Israel will grow to (Gen. 22:17). The shrewd businessmen had readily taken advantage of the many opportunities that were afforded for profit, as Assyria expanded its empire, but profit was all they were interested in. **Like locusts they strip the land and then fly away**. Once locusts have consumed the vegetation in an area, they move on. The traders were acting only in self-interest, and once there was no profit to be made from a place they left it. There may perhaps here be a hint that Nineveh itself will become so devastated that her trading community will leave her too. There will be no profits for them in the rubble.

Bureaucratic Collapse (3:17). The imagery of the locust is then applied in yet another way. **Your guards are like locusts, your officials like swarms of locusts** (*verse 17*). But the comparison is not only with the numbers of high-ranking officials that settled throughout the empire as locusts **settle in the walls on a cold day**. It is the fact that they are ever ready to move away when conditions are more favourable for them elsewhere. **When the sun appears they fly away, and no one knows where**. The army and bureaucracy of Nineveh will act in self-interest, just as they have done all along. When danger approaches the capital, they will find it suits them to move away. Many of the administrators seem in fact to have moved to Haran in the closing stages of the capture of Nineveh. The strength of the enemy was not the only factor contributing to her downfall; the lack of commitment in the army and bureaucracy was significant also.

Nahum turns to address the king of Assyria, and as he does so, he traces even higher up in society the complacency and corruption that had set in in Nineveh. **O king of Assyria, your shepherds slumber; your nobles lie down to rest** (*verse 18*). 'Shepherd' was a term used throughout the Ancient Near East to describe one who had the responsibility for ruling and governing a nation. Nahum here deftly ties together their previous easy-going attitudes ('the carefree city', Zeph. 2:15), and the fate that came upon them in consequence. They had whiled away their time in ease, neglectful of their duties, and so their slumber and rest has turned into 'their last sleep' (Psalm 76:5), from which they will not awaken (Jer. 51:39,57). These words seem to envisage the situation after the capture of the city, and the king would be Ashur-uballit who tried for a few years to keep the Assyrian empire going in Haran.

As he looked around him, he would find that Nahum's words had come true. **Your people are scattered on the mountains with no one to gather them**. It would have been the duty of the nobility to give a lead in bringing the people together, but they have been killed, and the people dispersed without effective leadership to organise them.

Nothing can heal your wound; your injury is fatal (*verse 19*). The wound is that of the king, but it refers to the devastation that has come upon his land, and especially his capital. He has lost control, and the situation cannot be recovered. Nineveh lay in the dust, never to recover, its very location uncertain for centuries.

Everyone who hears the news about you claps his hands at your fall. No doubt, many of Assyria's subject people did gloat over their misfortune at the hands of the Babylonians (Zephaniah 2:15). They had suffered so much from them that there would inevitably be rejoicing at their downfall. **Who has not felt your endless cruelty?**

But the rejoicing of the people of God will not be tainted by gloating. The focus of their joy is in the fact that the overthrow of evil vindicates the righteousness of God, and the removal of their enemies fulfils the promise of protection and deliverance he has given to them. Their faith in him has been justified (Rev. 19:1-3).

It is a warning also to others who resist him. He once sent a Jonah to Nineveh, with the message, 'Forty more days and Nineveh will be overturned' (Jonah 3:4). Then they had turned from their evil ways and were spared. But now the injury is fatal. Matters can be left too late. The plea to return to God is addressed not only to individuals, but also to nations and civilisations. If it is unheeded, there is a day of reckoning coming which shall vindicate God and bring ruin to those who persist in rebellion against him.

Study Guide

Nahum 1

verse 2: Is the concept of 'jealousy' appropriate in describing God today? (Deuteronomy 6:15; Joshua 24:19; 1 Kings 14:22; Joel 2:18; Zechariah 1:14; 8:2; Romans 8:38,39; Hebrews 13:5)

What is meant by God taking vengeance? (Psalm 94:1-11; Isaiah 59:18; Romans 12:19)

verse 3: Why can God not let the guilty go unpunished? (Isaiah 2:12-17; 37:23,29; Daniel 5:22-24; Romans 2:6; 2 Corinthians 5:10; 2 Thessalonians 1:8)

verse 7: How does God care for his people? (Psalms 25:4-6; 46:1; 59:16; Romans 8:32; 2 Corinthians 3:5; 12:9)

verse 9: What happens when human strategies conflict with God's plan? (Psalms 2:1; 21:11; Proverbs 21:30; Isaiah 8:10; Luke 12:16-21)

verse 15: What does the use of the same words here and in Isaiah 52:7 and Romans 10:15 tell us about the unity of Scripture and the on-going purposes of God?

Nahum 2

verse 2: How does the LORD restore his people's fortunes? (Isaiah 44:26; Jeremiah 30:3; 33:10,11; Zephaniah 3:20; Acts 3:21; 1 Peter 5:10)

verse 13: In the fall of Nineveh we see the LORD's opposition to a city that was full of evil. Later the same would be true of Babylon. To what extent can we find here a foreshadowing of the fall of the final Babylon (Revelation 18)?

Nahum 3

verse 1: By what standard does God judge human actions? (Isaiah 3:11; 65:6; Ezekiel 18:20; Matthew 16:27; 2 Corinthians 5:10; Revelation 22:12)

verse 5: Why are all nations accountable to God, even if they do not profess to be Christian? (Psalm 75:7,8; Proverbs 8:15,16; Daniel 2:21; John 19:11; 1 Timothy 6:15; 1 Peter 2:14)

verse 8: How may a false sense of security arise? (Psalms 20:7; 49:6,13,18; Proverbs 14:12; 16:2; 30:12; Jeremiah 23:17; Luke 12:15-21,33; James 1:26)

verse 11: How does Scripture evaluate human expedients to find safety? (Psalms 20:7; 33:17; Proverbs 21:31; Isaiah 30:1-5; Obadiah 3,4)

verse 19: How should we react when we hear of the downfall of those who have been enemies of the LORD?